About this Learning Guide

Shmoop Will Make You a Better Lover*
*of Literature, History, Poetry, Life...

Our lively learning guides are written by experts and educators who want to show your brain a good time. Shmoop writers come primarily from Ph.D. programs at top universities, including Stanford, Harvard, and UC Berkeley.

Want more Shmoop? We cover literature, poetry, bestsellers, music, US history, civics, biographies (and the list keeps growing). Drop by our website to see the latest.

www.shmoop.com

Table of Contents

Introduction

In a Nutshell

The Importance of Being Earnest, Oscar Wilde's last and most famous play, debuted in London on February 14, 1895. Wilde's fans wildly anticipated this new play and sunk their fangs into any breaking news of it. To protect his work-in-progress from prying eyes, Wilde's company gave it the working title *Lady Lancing*, who is mentioned once in Act III of the play.

At the time, Wilde was at the height of his success. But just a few months later his boyfriend's father sent an insulting letter calling him a "somdomite" – yep, he misspelled it. A humiliating trial was set in motion, and Wilde was convicted of "gross indecency" and sentenced to two years of hard labor.

"Life is too important a thing ever to talk seriously about it," wrote Wilde in one of his first plays, *Vera* or *The Nihilists*. Long interested in the combination of the serious with the trivial, Oscar Wilde experimented with different proportions of each in his plays like a baker trying to get the perfect sugar to salt ratio in chocolate chip cookies. By the time Wilde wrote *The Importance of Being Earnest* he had perfected his recipe.

The Importance of Being Earnest is funny all the time. There is nothing earnest about this play, at least on the surface. It's a satire of the Victorian era, when an intricate code of behavior governed everything from communication to sexuality. The most important rules applied to marriage – always a popular topic in Victorian plays, and one that interested Wilde, who was married to a woman but sexually involved with men.

During the Victorian period, marriage was about protecting your resources, and keeping socially unacceptable impulses under control. We can see this at work in the *The Importance of Being Earnest*, usually when the social referee, Lady Bracknell, blows her whistle. Her two main concerns are class and money. Jack is a no-go because he doesn't know who his parents are (i.e., his class is unknown). Lady Bracknell is concerned that he might be a butler in disguise who will squander her daughter Gwendolen's wealth. One character in particular, Cecily, becomes a lot more interesting when her fortune is mentioned. The ridiculous end of the play – three engagements in five minutes – is a "happy" one because everyone gets together. But think about it – they only get together because their social and economic fitness for each other is demonstrated.

Why Should I Care?

Who are the people in *The Importance of Being Earnest*, who do they want to be, and how does the identity they choose affect their choice of a spouse? Generally speaking, the characters are young, unattached people looking for the future. They have the ability to define themselves. Jack knows nothing about his past. Algernon can't remember what his father looked like and says they weren't on speaking terms. Cecily is an orphan, creating herself in a diary full of fictitious events. Jack and Algernon are ready to change their names. Only Gwendolen has a

strong link to the past (i.e., to Lady Bracknell). With perhaps the exception of Gwendolen, these characters could choose to recreate themselves in a unique and unconventional way.

But they don't. According to Wilde: if you give a person an opportunity to invent himself, he will choose to be exactly who he should, according to social rules.

What a relief we don't live in Victorian England. No rules in America, man, it's the land of the free! Be who you want to be.

Really? There are no expectations? No unspoken rules? No opportunities to disappoint your family with your choices – of school, of career, of romantic partner? Maybe there are expectations and rules after all. The question of how much control we have over our identity – and the life path that comes with it – is still incredibly relevant to us today.

Book Summary

Algernon Moncrieff welcomes his friend Ernest Worthing in for a visit. Through an incident with a cigarette case and an unlucky inscription, Ernest is forced to confess that his name is really Jack. The story goes like this: in the country, Jack must lead the boring life of responsible guardian for his pretty, young ward Cecily. So he made up a seedy younger brother named Ernest, who is the urban socialite.

Cecily, we learn, is a bit too interested in Ernest for her own good. Whenever Jack feels like it, he visits London on the pretense that he's cleaning up Ernest's messes. After all, as the older brother he must be responsible for getting his younger brother out of trouble. Instead, Jack takes on the name Ernest and goes partying around town. Algernon is amused by this discovery and reveals that he has a similar nonexistent friend. Algernon's friend is a perpetual invalid named Bunbury, who allows Algernon to visit the country whenever he likes.

We learn that Jack is in love with Gwendolen Fairfax, who is Algernon's cousin and coincidentally scheduled to visit that day. (Both Algernon and Gwendolen think that Jack's name is Ernest.) Jack cuts a deal with Algernon; if Algernon can get Gwendolen's mother, Lady Bracknell, out of the room, then Jack can propose to Gwendolen. In return, Jack will dine with Algernon tonight so that Algernon will avoid dining with his Aunt Augusta (a.k.a. Lady Bracknell).

The plan works. We learn that Gwendolen is smitten by the name, Ernest. She is just accepting Ernest's proposal when Lady Bracknell re-enters the room, discovers them, and furiously sends Gwendolen down to the carriage. Lady Bracknell gives Ernest a chance to prove his worthiness by interviewing him. Once she decides that he is not fit for her daughter, she makes it clear that Gwendolen is not engaged to Ernest.

In a way, it is ironic that Lady Bracknell doesn't approve of the engagement to Ernest. Ernest is rich, has a good reputation around town, and seems to be perfectly suitable for Gwendolen.

Except for one thing: he's an orphan, abandoned at birth for unknown reasons, and found in a handbag at Victoria train station. This doesn't fly with Lady Bracknell, who tells him to find his parents ASAP and then dismisses him. Furious, Jack and Algernon concoct a scheme for getting rid of Ernest. They decide that he'll die in Paris of a severe chill.

In the meantime, Gwendolen has found an opportunity to slip back into the room and confess her undying love for Ernest. Having heard her mother's furious remarks, she's fascinated about his mysterious background and asks for his country address. As Ernest gives it, Algernon discreetly copies it down and later announces to his servant that he's going Bunburying tomorrow.

At Jack's country estate, young Cecily does everything she can to avoid studying her German grammar. She lies to get her governess, Miss Prism, to take a break. Miss Prism allows this only because she's distracted by Dr. Chasuble, the local reverend. Just as Miss Prism leaves, the arrival of Ernest Worthing is announced. It turns out to be Algernon. Algernon and Cecily flirt outrageously. Cecily reveals that she's been fantasizing about Earnest for quite some time, and has even imagined that she's engaged to him. She invites him in for dinner.

At that moment, Miss Prism and Dr. Chasuble return from their walk, only to meet Jack dressed in black mourning clothes. He's come home early to announce that his brother, Ernest, has died tragically in Paris, of a severe chill.

Right on cue, Cecily comes out to tell her Uncle Jack that Ernest has come to visit. When Jack sees it's Algernon, he is furious and arranges for Ernest to leave via the dog-cart. When the cart comes, Algernon promptly sends it away. Cecily pays Algernon a visit and they engage in more flirtation, where we learn that Cecily is obsessed with the name, "Ernest."

When Algernon leaves (to arrange a baptism), Gwendolen arrives. Cecily entertains her. When each lady learns that the other is supposedly engaged to Ernest Worthing, they immediately start fighting. Luckily, both Jack and Algernon show up in time to clear up any doubt. Their true identities are revealed, as well as the fact that there is no Ernest. The women, realizing they've been tricked, suddenly become as close as sisters and go up to the house arm-in-arm, turning their backs on the men. Meanwhile, the men take out their frustration on the remaining tea items, fighting over the muffins, while they figure out what to do.

Eventually, they enter the house, and confess to the women. The Ernest business, they say, was done only so that they could see their beloved ladies as often as possible. The women forgive them. But their joy is interrupted by the arrival of Lady Bracknell. She has come to bring Gwendolen home. When she sees Cecily holding Algernon's hand, she gives her an icy glare, but politely asks Jack how big this girl's inheritance is. When she finds out that the girl is extremely wealthy, Lady Bracknell's attitude toward Cecily changes and she gives consent for her and Algernon to marry. But Jack, as Cecily's guardian, refuses to give *his* consent unless Lady Bracknell allows him to marry Gwendolen. Lady Bracknell wants nothing to do with it.

Dr. Chasuble shows up to tell Jack and Algernon that everything is ready for their baptisms and happens to mention Miss Prism. Lady Bracknell's ears prick up at the name. Miss Prism is brought before her and shamefacedly confesses the truth: she was once Lady Bracknell's

servant and was in charge of a certain child. One day, she took the baby out in his stroller for a walk and brought along some leisure reading– a three-volume novel that she had written – and kept in a handbag. Distracted, she switched the two – putting the novel in the stroller and the baby into the hand bag. She dropped the handbag off at Victoria train station.

At this discovery, Jack freaks out and runs upstairs to find something. When he comes back down, he's holding the handbag (remember, Jack is an orphan who was found in a handbag). Jack mistakenly thinks Miss Prism is his mother, but is corrected by Lady Bracknell, who tells him that a Mrs. Moncrieff is his mother. That makes Jack Algernon's older brother.

Then, they all wonder what Jack's real name is. Remember, Gwendolen will only love him if his name is Ernest. Lady Bracknell tells Jack he was named after his father, but nobody can remember what the General's name was. Jack looks up "Moncrieff" in his book of Army Lists. The results? His father's name was Ernest. So he's been telling the truth all along. His name really is Ernest. And now he can marry Gwendolen. There's general rejoicing. Gwendolen hugs Ernest. Cecily hugs Algernon. Miss Prism hugs Dr. Chasuble. And Ernest closes the play by insisting that he's now learned the "importance of being earnest."

Act I

- Let's set the scene: Lane, Algernon's servant, is arranging tea on the table in his luxurious morning-room. We hear the sound of piano music in the next room. After it falls silent, Algernon enters.
- Algernon checks that Lane has ordered the cucumber sandwiches for Lady Bracknell. When Lane hands them to him, Algernon takes some and flops down on the sofa. They talk about drinking and married life.
- Finishing his duties, Lane leaves the room.
- To himself, Algernon remarks that Lane's view about marriage are "lazy."
- Algernon comments he thinks it should be the job of the "lower classes" (I.17) to demonstrate good behavior for everyone else.
- His thoughts are interrupted by Lane, who announces the arrival of Mr. Ernest Worthing.
- The two friends discuss where Ernest has been and what activities he's been up to.
- Ernest claims he was in the country.
- Doubtful about that, Algy tests Ernest – asking if he was in Shropshire. Ernest seems confused, then stutters yes, he was in Shropshire. Uncomfortable, Ernest quickly changes the subject.
- Algernon reveals that Aunt Augusta and Gwendolen are coming for tea, but that Aunt Augusta won't be happy that Ernest is here because he flirts disgracefully with Gwendolen.
- Ernest protests that he's in love with Gwendolen and has come to town specifically to propose to her.
- Algernon is startled. "I thought you'd come up for pleasures?...I call that business" (I.37).
- Algy kindly comments that he doesn't think Ernest will ever marry Gwendolen.
- When Ernest asks why not, Algy replies that girls never marry the men they flirt with. Plus, Algy says he doesn't give his consent – Gwen is his first cousin.
- Algernon follows up: Ernest still hasn't explained the Cecily situation to him.

- Ernest claims that he doesn't know of any Cecily.
- Algernon is perplexed, and decides to pull out his secret weapon; he summons Lane to get the cigarette case Ernest left on his last visit.
- Now Ernest has some explaining to do.
- There's an inscription inside the cigarette case that says: "From little Cecily with her fondest love to her dear Uncle Jack" (I.68).
- Algernon plays with Ernest, asking him pointed questions about this mysterious Cecily while Ernest chases him around the room, grabbing for his cigarette case.
- Ernest tries to get out of his sticky situation by claiming Cecily his aunt and a short woman, which would explain the "little" part. (Actually Jack offers a witty reply that you should definitely check out in the play.)
- In the end, the truth is revealed.
- Ernest's name is not really Ernest. It's Jack. Actually, he explains: it's "Ernest" in town and "Jack" in the country. Algernon thinks this reply makes total sense. He then exclaims that he knew Ernest/Jack was a Bunburyist.
- When Algernon finally gives back the incriminating cigarette case, Jack tells the truth. (Yes, his name is really Jack.)
- Here's the deal: when he was a little boy, Jack's adopted guardian Mr. Thomas Cardew wrote in his will that I was to be the guardian of his granddaughter, Miss Cecily Cardew. Little Cecily calls Jack "Uncle" out of "motives of respect that you could not possibly appreciate" (I.79). She lives out in my country house with her governess, Miss Prism.
- When Algernon tries to find out where this country house is, Jack curtly says that's none of his business, but it's most definitely not in Shropshire.
- Jack explains why he has two different names.
- Jack is a very moral and boring legal guardian in the country. Jack invented Ernest, who is supposedly his troublesome little brother. Ernest's scandalous doings in the city give Jack an excuse to leave the country, (on the pretense of clearing up Ernest's mess), to go to town.
- Delighted, Algernon exclaims that Jack is really a "Bunburyist" and, when he sees Jack's puzzled expression, now it's time for Algernon to explain.
- Like Jack, Algernon has invented a useful residing-in-the-country pal named Bunbury who is "an invaluable permanent invalid" (I.88). Because of Bunbury, Algernon always has an excuse to get out of social engagements.
- In fact, Algernon explains, Bunbury was the reason that he's able to dine with Jack tonight at Willis's. (This dinner date is to get out of dining with Aunt Augusta.)
- Jack protests that he never invited Algy to dinner, but Algernon pleads with him to come because he's too embarrassed and bored to dine with his family.
- Jack goes back to the original topic and protests that he's not a Bunburyist since he intends to kill off Ernest very conveniently if Gwendolen accepts his proposal.
- Besides, Jack continues, Cecily is a little too interested in Ernest. Which is polite parent talk for "she has a crush on him."
- Suddenly, the bell rings, signaling that Aunt Augusta has arrived.
- Algernon quickly cuts a deal with Jack: if Algernon e can get Aunt Augusta (a.k.a. Lady Bracknell) away from Gwendolen for ten minutes so that Jack can propose, Jack will dine with him tonight at Willis's as compensation. Jack agrees.
- Lane enters to announce the arrival of Lady Bracknell and Miss Fairfax (a.k.a. Gwendolen).
- Algernon goes forward to greet his guests. Lady Bracknell is icily cold and polite to Jack,

- but Gwendolen starts flirting with him immediately.
- When Lady Bracknell asks for the promised cucumber sandwiches, Algernon finds – to his horror – that he's eaten all of them without noticing.
- Algernon and Lane improvise, putting on a charade that there were no cucumbers to be found at market that morning, "not even for ready money" (I.118).
- Lady Bracknell takes the missing sandwiches kindly since she's already had crumpets with a friend, Lady Harbury. But she doesn't take it so well when Algernon informs her he's not dining with her tonight, since poor Bunbury is sick again.
- Lady Bracknell remarks that it's irresponsible for someone to be so unhealthy. She orders Algernon to tell Mr. Bunbury to be well on Saturday because she needs Algernon to arrange the music at her last party of the season.
- Soon, Algernon and Lady Bracknell proceed into the next room to review the music arrangements Algernon has prepared.
- Gwendolen, disobeying her mother's orders, stays behind to talk to Jack.
- Jack, with Gwendolen's encouragement, loses no time in confessing his ardent and undying love for her. She reciprocates, calling him "my own Ernest!" (I.145)
- We learn that Gwendolen has always had a fantasy about marrying a man named Ernest.
- This is a problem for Jack. So he asks if she really couldn't love him if his name wasn't Ernest? He suggests the charming name, Jack, for example.
- When Gwendolen scoffs, Jack suggests that "I must get christened – I mean we must get married at once" (I.154).
- Gwendolen protests that he has not proposed yet. Jack doesn't hesitate. And Gwendolen accepts.
- But here comes trouble. Lady Bracknell enters and, horrified, orders Jack to "rise...from this semi-recumbent posture" because "it is most indecorous" (I.168).
- Gwendolen tries to stop her mother, protesting that Jack isn't finished yet.
- When Lady Bracknell learns of their engagement, things get messy. She reminds Gwendolen that "when you do become engaged to someone, I, or your father...will inform you of the fact" (I.172).
- Lady Bracknell commands Gwendolen to wait for her in the carriage outside. Down-spirited, Gwendolen obeys.
- Lady Bracknell interrogates Jack.
- She tells him he's not on her list of eligible young men, but she might change her mind if he answers her questions satisfactorily. She makes notes in her book as she asks questions.
- Does he smoke? Yes. She's pleased since men should always have some sort of "occupation."
- How old is he? Twenty-nine. Lady Bracknell has no problem with his age.
- Does he know everything or nothing? Nothing. She's delighted to hear that his "natural ignorance" (I.184) is preserved.
- How much does he make? Seven to eight thousand pounds a year in investments. But, Jack hastens to add, he does have both nice country and town houses. This answer is satisfactory.
- What's his town address? 149 Belgrave Square. Lady Bracknell disproves of the address, but that can change.
- What is his political party? Liberal Unionist. Well, that "counts as being a Tory" (I.200).
- Just when we think Jack's got it in the bag, Lady Bracknell asks the tough questions.

- Are his parents living? He's lost both his parents.
- She is appalled and asks who his father was. Jack doesn't know. He explains that he was an orphan, found in a hand bag at Victoria Station by a gentleman named Thomas Cardew.
- Lady Bracknell is not happy to hear this news. She declares his good social standing is in severe question.
- She advises him to try to "acquire some relations as soon as possible, and to make a definite effort to produce at any rate one parent, of either sex, before the season is quite over" (I.216).
- With that, he is dismissed.
- From the other room, clueless Algy starts playing the *Wedding March* on the piano. Jack is furious.
- The interrogation conveniently gives both of the men a chance to rant about Lady Bracknell, a rant which ends in Jack's uncomfortable realization that Gwendolen might end up just like her mother.
- When Algernon slyly asks if Jack told Gwendolen the truth of his double identities, Jack indignantly replies that "the truth isn't quite the sort of thing one tells to a nice, sweet, refined girl" (I.236).
- In an effort to make himself seem more acceptable to Lady Bracknell, Jack conjures up a plan to have his brother Ernest die of a severe chill in Paris by the end of the week.
- When Algernon interrupts that the news of Ernest's death will devastate Cecily, Jack replies that it'll be good for her.
- Algy remarks offhand that he'd like to meet Cecily, but Jack is adamant that he never will because Cecily is "excessively pretty" and "only just eighteen" (I.248).
- Jack thinks that if Cecily ever meets Gwendolen they would be great friends, but Algy is more skeptical.
- As they're figuring out what to do for the rest of the evening, Gwendolen enters unaccompanied. She asks Algernon to turn his back so she can something privately to Ernest.
- She admits that Lady Bracknell will not let her marry Ernest, but Gwen promises she'll always love him. She admits that the story of his "romantic origin" has "naturally stirred the deeper fibres of [her] nature" (I.272).
- She asks for his country house address. As Jack recites it to her, Algernon stealthily copies it down on his shift-cuff. He tells her he's only in the country until Monday, and then accompanies her out to her carriage.
- Algernon is left alone with Lane, who brings him his daily mail. Algernon announces that he's going Bunburying tomorrow and will not be back until Monday.
- Algernon starts laughing in delight, only to be interrupted by the returning Jack. When Jack asks why Algy is laughing, Algernon jokes that he's worried about Bunbury.
- As Jack leaves, Algernon glances at his shirt-cuff and smiles.

Act II

- The setting is the garden in the Manor House – Jack's country estate. It's July. A table full

- of books is set up beneath a yew tree in the rose garden. Miss Prism is sitting at the table while Cecily is in the back, watering the flowers.
- Miss Prism calls to Cecily to stop doing such a mundane task as watering the flowers because she needs to do her German grammar lesson.
- Cecily argues that she doesn't want to because she knows she looks plain after her German lesson.
- Miss Prism retorts that Uncle Jack is only looking out for Cecily's education.
- Cecily complains that Uncle Jack is so serious.
- Miss Prism defends him as the pinnacle of "duty and responsibility" (II.5). She adds that he's even helping out that unfortunately troublesome younger brother of his.
- This piques Cecily's interest and she wishes aloud that Uncle Jack would bring Ernest by sometime so that Miss Prism could reform him.
- She begins writing in her diary, where she keeps all the "wonderful secrets of [her] life" (II.10). At this, Miss Prism comments that she was once a writer herself.
- She wrote a three-volume novel (the bane of Cecily's existence) back in the day. Miss Prism tells Cecily to work on her lesson.
- But the perfect excuse to ignore the lesson is just arriving – Dr. Chasuble. At the sight of him, Miss Prism blushes and stands.
- They're so obviously crushing on each other that Cecily finds it easy to persuade them to take a walk together.
- While they're out, Merriman the butler tells Cecily that a Mr. Ernest Worthing has just arrived.
- Cecily is overjoyed to finally be able to meet the infamous Ernest, but she's scared at the same time.
- Algernon enters, disguised as Ernest. He greets his "cousin," Cici. They talk about how "wicked" he is, with Cecily making comments about how he should reform himself.
- Charmingly, Algernon/Ernest asks Cecily to try to reform him that very afternoon.
- As they're flirting and Ernest is finding every way possible to compliment Cecily, like asking for a pink rose for his button-hole "because you are like a pink rose, cousin Cecily" (II.75).
- Algernon learns that Jack plans to send Ernest to Australia.
- As Cecily's putting a flower into his buttonhole, Miss Prism and Dr. Chasuble return, discussing the moral advantages and disadvantages of marriage. They're so wrapped up in each other that they don't realize that Cecily is not where they left her.
- Before they can send out a search party, Jack arrives home, dressed in a black suit of mourning.
- When they ask him about it, Jack announces that he's returned early because his brother Ernest is dead. He died last night in Paris of a "severe chill."
- When Dr. Chasuble offers to perform a funeral ceremony for Ernest, Jack suddenly remembers something. He asks Dr. Chasuble if he can be christened. After some questions, Dr. Chasuble relents and they arrange for Jack to come by at half-past five that evening.
- Cecily comes from the house to meet her Uncle Jack with the happy news that his brother Ernest arrived just recently and is now in the dining-room.
- Jack is completely confused.
- Dr. Chasuble – trying to smooth over the awkward situation – says that these are good tidings indeed (that Ernest is alive and all). The mystery is solved when Jack sees

Algernon sitting at the table.

- Jack refuses to shake hands with Algernon. We learn from Cecily that Ernest has been telling her about his poor friend, Mr. Bunbury.
- Finally, Cecily declares she will never speak to Uncle Jack again if he doesn't shake hands with Ernest. Jack gives in reluctantly and Miss Prism praises Cecily for her wonderful act of kindness today. They leave Jack and Ernest together.
- Furiously, Jack tells Algy to leave at once. But he's interrupted when Merriman comes in to reveal that Mr. Ernest's luggage has been put in the bedroom next to Jack's.
- Jack tells Merriman that unfortunately Ernest's dog-cart has arrived to take him away; he's been called back to town.
- While Jack rants at Algernon, Algernon talks about how pretty Cecily is. Jack declares the dog-cart is here and leaves, just in time to miss Algy's comment that he has fallen in love with Cecily.
- Cecily appears with a watering can in her hand. She and Ernest/Algernon exchange glances. She pleads with Merriman to let Ernest stay for another five minutes.
- Algernon informs her that Jack is sending him away and compliments her beauty. Flattered, Cecily begins copying his words down in her diary, but refuses to let him look at it.
- When the dog-cart comes again, Ernest tells it to come again next week.
- Without ceremony, he asks Cecily to marry him. She responds amusedly that they've been engaged for months.
- She confides her past fantasies to him, as they're written in her diary. Apparently, Ernest proposed on Valentine's day but they'd broken it off a month later. Now they're back together, which she can prove with the many love letters from him that she has saved (and written herself).
- Ernest kisses her for being so forgiving.
- Then she confides that it's always been a "girlish dream of mine to love someone whose name was Ernest" (II.233).
- Distraught, he asks her if she could love him under any other name…say…Algernon, for instance.
- Cecily finds it a rather aristocratic name, but no, she wouldn't be able to love him then.
- At that declaration, Ernest/Algernon promptly begins asking her about the rector and whether or not he performs christenings.
- Algernon leaves to find Dr. Chasuble about a very important matter. As he leaves, Cecily comments that she likes his hair so much.
- Soon, Merriman enters to tell Cecily that a Miss Fairfax has arrived to see Mr. Worthing.
- Cecily invites Miss Fairfax to sit with her until Uncle Jack comes out.
- They're both such charming girls that when they meet, they declare they'll be best friends and call each other immediately by their first names.
- They talk for a little while before Gwendolen works up the balls to ask Cecily if she can inspect her.
- Gwendolen, peering through her glasses, finds Cecily rather too attractive and loudly wishes that she were a bit older and more decidedly more dowdy. She asks about Cici's relations and finds out that Mr. Worthing is Cecily's guardian.
- Now that's problematic, Gwendolen says, since Ernest never mentioned it to her.
- When Cecily hears the name Ernest, she quickly explains the situation.
- It's not Ernest Worthing who is my guardian, she says sweetly, but his older brother, Jack.

- That's a relief to Gwendolen, who suddenly becomes polite again.
- Cecily proudly declares that she's going to be Ernest Worthing's wife.
- Gwendolen rises to her feet. Excuse me? You're mistaken. Ernest proposed to me yesterday. Cecily retorts that he must've changed his mind because he just proposed to her ten minutes ago. The two women eye each other coldly before Gwendolen announces – alluding to Cecily's rude manners – that they obviously move in different social circles.
- Right before they can start clawing at each other, Merriman comes by to arrange their tea things. The girls bite back their acidic words in his presence.
- As Merriman serves them, they glare at each other but chitchat in cordial tones. However, their small talk bristles with little insults, mostly about the superiority of urban life (from Gwendolen) vs. the superiority of country life (from Cecily).
- When Cecily serves Gwendolen tea, she serves it in the opposite manner that Gwendolen requests – giving her lots of sugar in her tea and cake instead of bread & butter.
- Thank goodness, Jack arrives just in time to break up their fight.
- When Gwendolen jumps on him and asks if he's to be married to Cecily, Jack laughs it off and kisses Gwendolen.
- The truth comes out. Cecily replies that he's not Ernest Worthing; that's Uncle Jack.
- At the unglamorous name, Gwendolen recoils in disgust.
- Right on cue, Algernon enters and Cecily goes through the same routine with him. When he confirms he's not to be married to Gwendolen, she allows him to kiss her.
- This time it's Gwendolen's turn to clear up the confusion. She reveals that he's not Ernest Worthing; it's Algernon Moncrieff, her cousin.
- Cecily backs away when she hears "Algernon."
- The two women embrace each other in distress, while the men hang their heads in shame.
- They finally ask Jack who Ernest is and he is forced to admit that Ernest doesn't exist.
- When both girls realize with horror that neither of them are engaged to anyone, they agree to go into the house where the men won't dare to follow them. With scornful looks, they leave.
- Infuriated and frustrated, the two men turn on each other for the horrible results of their Bunburying.
- Both blame each other for deceiving the girls. They argue for a while and Algernon sits down agitatedly and begins to eat the muffins left by the ladies.
- Jack comments that it's heartless for him to eat so calmly when they're in such a state and begins fighting with him over the muffins.
- In the midst of their squabbling, each discovers that the other has a christening to attend that evening to be named Ernest. Their christenings are scheduled only fifteen minutes apart!
- Both try to dissuade each other from doing so, without success.
- The act ends with both guys still munching muffins and bickering with each other.

Act III

- Gwendolen and Cecily are seeking sanctuary in the morning room at the Manor House. They peer out the window in curiosity at the two men.

- The girls notice that the men haven't followed them into the house and are eating muffins. They're worried that the guys don't seem to be noticing them at all.
- A moment later, when the two guys start walking towards the house, the women are affronted and agree to give them the silent treatment.
- But that soon falls apart. Cecily breaks her silence to ask Algernon why he pretended to be Jack's brother. He answers candidly – to "have an opportunity of meeting you" (III.15). Cecily melts.
- Then it's Gwendolen's turn. She asks Jack why he pretended to have a brother. Before he can answer, she suggests that it was possibly so that he could have an excuse to come up to town to see her as often as possible. He confirms it.
- Satisfied, the girls confide to forgive the men. But there's a still a problem. The girls confront the guys in loud unison: "Your Christian names are still an insuperable barrier. That is all!" (III.29)
- In other words, the girls can't possibly marry them if their names aren't Ernest.
- In response, the men answer in unison: "Our Christian names! Is that all? But we are going to be christened this afternoon" (III.30).
- Seeing that their beloveds are brave enough to endure such a harrowing ordeal as a christening for their sake, rush into their lovers' arms.
- Merriman enters, sees all the hugging going on, and coughs loudly. He announces the arrival of Lady Bracknell. The startled couples separate.
- Lady Bracknell loses no time in asking Gwendolen just what she's doing. At the news that she's engaged to Jack, Lady Bracknell turns her wrath on him. She orders that all communication between them must stop immediately and ignores his protests.
- Then she turns to Algernon and asks if this is where Bunbury resides. Caught by surprise, Algernon answers no, then stutters that Bunbury is actually dead. He died by exploding. Lady Bracknell is appalled by his method of death, considering it a "revolutionary outrage" (III.54) but is glad that the matter is settled.
- On to business. Lady Bracknell asks Jack who is that young person holding Algernon's hand so inappropriately.
- When she learns Algernon is engaged to Cecily, she comments that there must be something in the air here that is particularly exciting. Because the number of engagements here "seems to me considerably above the proper average that statistics have laid down for our guidance" (III.61).
- Slyly, she asks if Miss Cardew has any relations to the railway stations in London.
- Jack is fuming, but coldly answers no and recites Cecily's proper parents, plus their address. He assures her that she can find the same information in the Court Guides. And he lists off all the documentation he has of Cecily – including birth certificates, baptism records, incidents of illness and vaccinations.
- Lady Bracknell brushes them off, telling Gwendolen it's time to leave.
- As they exit, she asks offhand if Miss Cardew has any amount of fortune.
- Oh, Jack answers, just a hundred and thirty *thousand* pounds.
- Lady Bracknell freezes. Suddenly, Cecily looks much more attractive to her. With Cecily's eager cooperation, Lady Bracknell inspects her profile and declares she has "distinct social possibilities" (III.75). Finally, she gives her consent. She even allows Cecily to call her Aunt Augusta.
- But Jack has other ideas. As Cecily's legal guardian, he refuses to give consent for her to marry Algernon. When Lady Bracknell, insulted, asks what could possibly be wrong with

Algernon, Jack reveals that Algernon has lied – deceiving his whole family into thinking he was the nonexistent younger brother, Ernest.

- On top of that, Jack continues, he not only drank an entire bottle of his best wine, but also ate every single muffin at tea. Jack stands by his verdict; he won't give Algernon consent to marry Cecily.
- Lady Bracknell, however, has hope. After learning Cecily is eighteen, Lady Bracknell says it won't be long before she comes of age and she can make her own decisions.
- But Jack interrupts, saying her grandfather's will dictates she won't come of age until she's thirty-five.
- Although Lady Bracknell doesn't think the wait is that bad, Cecily is impatient and declares she can't wait that long.
- Finally, Jack deigns to negotiate: if Lady Bracknell will give consent for him to marry Gwendolen, he'll consent to let Algernon marry Cecily.
- Lady Bracknell flatly refuses and tells Gwendolen to get ready to go. They've already missed five trains back to town.
- Dr. Chasuble enters at this crucial moment to announce that everything is ready for the christenings. Lady Bracknell will not hear of such nonsense.
- Jack sadly agrees to call off the christenings, because there's no point now. Nobody is getting married.
- This news saddens Dr. Chasuble, but he's glad to have some free time this evening. He's heard that Miss Prism has been waiting for him in the vestry.
- Lady Bracknell starts at the name. Apparently they have a history.
- Jack tries to explain that Miss Prism is Cecily's esteemed governess. But this has no impact on Lady Bracknell. She orders Chasuble to send for Miss Prism at once.
- At the sight of the stern Lady Bracknell, Miss Prism stops dead in her tracks, and turns around with the intention of running away.
- Prism! Lady Bracknell spits. Miss Prism approaches humbly.
- Lady Bracknell recites Prism's crime: Twenty-eight years ago, Miss Prism left Lord Bracknell's house with a perambulator (read: a baby stroller) containing a male child.
- Both of them disappeared without a trace. Weeks later, the police found the perambulator in Bayswater with an especially sappy three-volume novel inside. But the baby was gone.
- Prism, Lady Bracknell screeches, where is that baby?
- Shamed, Miss Prism confesses. She doesn't know where the child is, but she tells what happened the best she can. On that fateful day, she not only had the baby in the perambulator with her, but the prized three-volume novel she had written, contained in an old hang-bag.
- Later that day, she got confused and accidentally put the book into the perambulator and the baby into the handbag.
- Jack, who's been listening intently, asks where she sent the handbag. Miss Prism confesses she deposited it at a cloakroom in Victoria Station (presumably to be sent to a potential publisher), the Brighton line.
- At this news, Jack runs up to his room, leaving the others baffled. It sounds like things are being frantically thrown around.
- After some time, Jack returns with a black leather handbag. He asks Miss Prism to inspect it and decide whether or not it's the one she owned. After a few moments, Miss Prism declares that it is indeed hers. She points to the lock, which is engraved with her initials, as proof.

- Jack smiles and reveals that he was the baby inside the handbag. Then he impulsively hugs Miss Prism, screaming in joy, "Mother!" (III.148)
- But Miss Prism recoils, saying that she is not married. How could he dare insinuate such a thing? But Jack is in a generous mood and forgives her, only to hug her again.
- Stunned, Miss Prism detaches herself and points to Lady Bracknell. That woman, she says, can tell you who you really are.
- Lady Bracknell delivers the stunning news. "You are the son of my poor sister, Mrs. Moncrieff, and consequently Algernon's elder brother" (III.153).
- Jack is beside himself with joy, glad because this means that he had been telling the truth all these years; he does indeed have a younger brother. He grabs Algy and goes around the room, introducing each and every person to his "unfortunate brother," Algernon.
- Gwendolen finally asks the question that's been on our minds. What is Jack's real name? He must remember that his marriage depends on it.
- Jack turns to Lady Bracknell for the answer. She answers that he was indeed christened, and – as befits the eldest son – was named after his father. But, unfortunately, she cannot remember the General's name.
- Neither can Algy, because their father died when he was a baby.
- But Jack has an idea. His father's name would appear in the Army Lists, wouldn't it.
- Jack turns to the bookcase and tears out volumes until he finds the Army List he wants. He flips through the 'M's until he finds the Moncrieff entry. He reads out the Christian name: Ernest John.
- He shuts the book and turns to Gwendolen with the suspenseful news that his name really is Ernest. He hasn't been lying after all.
- Lady Bracknell now remembers that the General's name was Ernest. She knew she had a reason for disliking that name.
- This clears the way for a love-fest. Gwendolen rushes into Jack's arms. Dr. Chasuble (Frederick!) embraces Miss Prism (Laetitia!). Algernon sweeps Cecily off her feet.
- There's general chaotic joy.
- When Lady Bracknell tries to put a damper on things by saying Jack is "displaying signs of triviality" (III.180), Jack replies suavely that, on the contrary, "I've now realised for the first time in my life the vital importance of being earnest."

Themes

Theme of Lies and Deceit

The most prevalent reason characters in *The Importance of Being Earnest* lie is to get out of social or familial duties and, instead, to do something more enjoyable. Not surprisingly, few characters hold honesty in high regard. However, we see how hard it is for characters to set things straight once they've lied about them. As the situation gets increasingly complicated, characters must weave more complex lies to get out of the tangles of their previous lies. Eventually they reach the point where lies will no longer work and the truth is revealed. Perhaps the most striking thing is that none of the characters ever shows true remorse or guilt about lying.

Questions About Lies and Deceit

1. What is Jack's first lie? How does all the action of the play depend on this one lie? In other words, if Jack had told the truth at the beginning, would the rest of the play have been possible?
2. How do Algernon's lies complement Jack's lies? Does the similarity between Algernon and Jack's lies indicate that the two men are similar?
3. How do the women's lies compare to the men's? Are they as deceitful? What do the women lie about?
4. Why do the characters lie? If it is for love, do you think their lies are justified?

Chew on Lies and Deceit

In *The Importance of Being Earnest*, the men's lies are justified because they lie primarily so that they could spend time with the women they love.

In *The Importance of Being Earnest*, the men's lies are not justified because they lie primarily to get out of social responsibilities.

Theme of Marriage

The big question *The Importance of Being Earnest* raises is whether marriage is pleasurable or a restrictive social duty. In general, the older generation thinks of marriage as a means to an end, a way of maintaining or bettering your social position. If you want to get married, you submit to an interrogation: "State your name, rank, and serial number." The number that matters in this case, however, is your income; you better have bank. You also need to have an acceptable title, along with the parents to prove it. The hot-blooded youngsters think they are interested in love. One of the huge ironies in the play – and what makes it a satire of Victorian society – is that, in the end, nobody really breaks the rules. They color within the lines, and marry exactly the type of person their society are expects them to.

Questions About Marriage

1. How do Lady Bracknell's views of marriage compare to Jack's and Gwendolen's? What does she value in a marriage? In contrast, what do Jack and Gwendolen want?
2. What does Algernon think of marriage? Is it business or pleasure to him? Why? And how does Bunbury fit in to his view on marriage?
3. How do the ladies' opinions of marriage differ from the men's? Why are they so adamant that the men propose properly to them? How is this empowering to them?
4. What does Miss Prism's discussion of marriage with Dr. Chasuble reveal about her character? Consider Dr. Chasuble's position as a celibate clergyman.

Chew on Marriage

In *The Importance of Being Earnest*, Miss Prism and Dr. Chasuble challenge the social order by ultimately yielding to marriage based on love instead of marrying for social rank or wealth, as most of the older generation espouse.

In *The Importance of Being Earnest*, Algernon represents a modern mindset towards marriage because he is skeptical about the happiness of couples in marriage, and has fears about committing to one woman, unlike Jack – who holds more traditional nineteenth-century views on marriage.

Theme of Respect and Reputation

In this play, the upper classes care about being respectable – so much so that they do a lot of lying about it. In general, Victorian upper-class society holds slightly different expectations of men and women. Men need to be upstanding, rich, and from a good family. Women need to be upstanding, rich, from a good family, and chaste. Any deviation from the rules (being born poor, or being found in a handbag, in Jack's case) may prevent a young person from making a good match, and continuing his noble line.

Questions About Respect and Reputation

1. How is Jack and Gwendolen's behavior towards each other in public slightly disgraceful? How about Algernon and Cecily's? Who sets the standards of respectability for young couples?
2. Based on Lady Bracknell's interview with Jack, what qualities does the aristocracy require in suitors to their daughters? What about in potential daughter-in-laws? What does Lady Bracknell value about Cecily?
3. Which character – Jack or Algernon – has a more defined sense of respectability? How does this character reveal his ethics?
4. How is Miss Prism's holier-than-thou respectability mocked and parodied throughout the play? How does her hidden history undermine her pretentious words?

Chew on Respect and Reputation

The ultimate goal in *Earnest* is to reconcile romantic desires and respectability; in other words, Jack, Algernon, Gwendolen, and Cecily all strive to make their less-than-honorable courtship look appropriate to Lady Bracknell.

Although each character in *Earnest* strives to be respectable, none actually believes in the socially-proscribed standards, and all often mock the idea that one can be both respectable and happy.

Theme of Society and Class

The Importance of Being Earnest reveals the differences between the behavior of the upper class and that of the lower class. Members of the upper class display a great deal of pride and

pretense, feeling that they are inherently entitled to their wealth and higher social position. They are so preoccupied with maintaining the *status quo* that they quickly squash any signs of rebellion. In this play, Wilde satirizes the arrogance and hypocrisy of the aristocracy. The lower classes in *Earnest* are less pretentious and more humble, but equally good at making jokes.

Questions About Society and Class

1. Which character is the ultimate symbol of the aristocracy? Who is the symbol of a lower class? How does the former character treat the latter? What does this reveal about the aristocracy?
2. Compare the relationship of Lady Bracknell and Gwendolen to that of Jack and Cecily. Which pair has more trust between them? What does this say about family relationships in difference classes?
3. How do lower classes imitate the aristocracy? In daily life, what does Jack do to make himself more acceptable to Lady Bracknell? How about Cecily?
4. What is Wilde's attitude towards the aristocracy? Does he admire or make fun of them?

Chew on Society and Class

Although many of Wilde's characters in *Earnest* are aristocrats, he ultimately parodies the upper class's pride and pretension.

By imitating and trying to marry into the aristocracy, Jack is a hypocrite and a traitor to his own class.

Theme of Gender

In *The Importance of Being Earnest*, the question of each gender's role in society often centers on power. In the Victorian world of this play, men have greater influence than women. Men make the political decisions for their families, while women work around the house, quietly taking care of the children. Men are valued for their intellect and judgment, while women are attractive to men for their beauty and chastity. However, Wilde raises interesting questions about gender roles in *The Importance of Being Earnest*, by putting women (like Lady Bracknell) in positions of power and by showing that men (i.e., Jack and Algernon) can be irresponsible and bad at decision-making.

Questions About Gender

1. Based on their behavior towards Gwendolen and Cecily, what do Jack and Algernon value in women? How do the women's vanity add to this?
2. In contrast, what do Lady Bracknell and other respectable figures like Miss Prism value in men? How is this the same or different from what society values in women?
3. How do the major women in the play – Lady Bracknell, Gwendolen, and Cecily – reverse traditional gender roles? In contrast, how do they adhere to them?
4. How might Lady Bracknell's background and her history with Miss Prism mold her into a

powerful figure that completely overshadows Lord Bracknell?

Chew on Gender

In *Earnest*, figures like Lady Bracknell, Gwendolen, and Cecily reverse gender role stereotypes by exercising power and control over the opposite sex.

Although the female characters in *Earnest* exercise power briefly, they also conform to many female stereotypes – ultimately ensuring that the play upholds traditional gender stereotypes instead of challenging or changing them.

Theme of Versions of Reality: Romance

In *The Importance of Being Earnest*, pampered young women have a skewed sense of reality, inspired by romantic novels. When real life gets too boring, these women decide to take matters into their own hands by recording their fantasies in diaries. Potential lovers enter the picture and provide an opportunity to act out the fantasies, but the women's expectations of courtship often prove too whimsical and idealistic for reality. There's no tragic disillusionment here, though. Just marriages, and lots of them. *Earnest* is a comedy, after all.

Questions About Versions of Reality: Romance

1. How does a preference for the name, Ernest, provide the first hint that Gwendolen and Cecily are living in an idealized reality?
2. Where does Cecily record all her romantic fantasies? What qualities does a diary possess that make it an ideal medium for recording one's daydreams?
3. What is Miss Prism's definition of fiction? How does this apply to the girls' attitudes towards life?
4. Since we're on the topic of fantasy vs. reality, consider the inventions of Ernest and Bunbury. Then think about the women's whims. How do both the men and women in the play deal with reality?

Chew on Versions of Reality: Romance

Despite the happy ending of the *Earnest*, the character of Miss Prism shows the negative consequences that can result from trying to live a fictional romance in the real world; her history can be read as a warning to girls like Gwendolen and Cecily.

Characters of both sexes in *Earnest* invent fantasies – either through fictional characters or private novel-like worlds – to idealize and escape from the harsher realities of life.

Theme of Love

In *The Importance of Being Earnest*, it is often hard to distinguish Wilde's notion of romance from that of real love. Readers must settle for a decidedly un-modern definition of love. For

example, in *Earnest* physical beauty – both female and male – can initiate and sustain a love affair. Forgiveness is an ingredient of love as well. Both women forgive the men for their earlier deceptions when they discover the good intentions behind their crimes. It seems that the definition of love in this play is not so much unconditional and self-sacrificing love, but a general attitude of good intentions, admiration, and honest affection.

Questions About Love

1. How does each of our four main characters define love? How do their definitions of love coincide or clash with the ideals of fictional romance?
2. What initially attracts the women to the men? What initially attracts the men to women? Is this common for Victorian couples?
3. How do the men prove their love to the women? In return, how do the women show that their love for the men still survives?
4. In your opinion, which couple's love is more legitimate? Why?

Chew on Love

The concept of love in *Earnest* is never challenged; each of the four main characters complacently adores his or her lover purely for their looks or their names and never questions each other's character.

The integrity of each character's love in *Earnest* is challenged – both by the standards of high society and by the characters' own dishonesty – and all of them pass the test.

Theme of Foolishness and Folly

In *The Importance of Being Earnest*, the characters' foolishness is the core of the comedy. Often, we don't know whether a character says something contradictory or random in a serious way, or if the character is just joking. This ambiguity in tone makes readers both slightly uncomfortable and prone to laughter. Wilde shows his characters' folly in a number of ways: spinning something that is out of human control as if it were a simple matter of mundane choice, inverting aphorisms so that they mean the opposite of what common sense dictates, and simply juxtaposing random things so that they create an absurd situation.

Questions About Foolishness and Folly

1. Name three examples where characters say something paradoxical to give a comedic effect.
2. What is the effect of juxtaposing a serious situation (like having the girls leave the boys after discovering their deception) and a trivial one (like fighting over muffins) together? Can you think of other situations where juxtaposition creates a foolish and funny scene?
3. In your opinion, are the characters serious when they say things like "in all matters of grave importance, style, not sincerity is the vital thing"? (III.19) How does their ambiguity of tone make the situation funny? How does this logic drive the plot?

4. Consider all the characters. It seems they all have some foolish aspects. Which character, in your eyes, is the most foolish? Why?

Chew on Foolishness and Folly

In *The Importance of Being Earnest*, the crux of Wilde's humor depends on inversion of common sense and juxtaposition of random elements.

Lies and Deceit Quotes

Algernon: Yes; but this isn't your cigarette case. This cigarette case is a present from some one of the name of Cecily, and you said you didn't know any one of that name.

Jack: Well, if you want to know, Cecily happens to be my aunt.

[….]

Algernon: [Retreating to back of sofa] But why does she call herself little Cecily if she is your aunt and lives at Tunbridge Wells? [Reading] 'From little Cecily with her fondest love.'

Jack: [Moving to sofa and kneeling upon it] My dear fellow, what on earth is there in that? Some aunts are tall, some aunts are not tall. That is a matter that surely an aunt may be allowed to decide for herself. You seem to think that every aunt should be exactly like your aunt! That is absurd! For Heaven's sake give me back my cigarette case. [Follows Algernon round the room .]

Algernon: Yes. But why does your aunt call you her uncle? 'From little Cecily, with her fondest love to her dear Uncle Jack.' There is no objection, I admit, to an aunt being a small aunt, but why an aunt, no matter what her size may be, should call her own nephew her uncle, I can't quite make out. Besides, your name isn't Jack at all; it is Ernest.

Jack: It isn't Ernest; it's Jack. (I.62-69)

Thought: Jack lies to cover up his double life. A simple white lie that he doesn't know anyone named "Cecily" gets him into an incredibly messy situation. When he's forced to admit he does know a "Cecily," he tries to pass her off as his aunt. But Algy, a fellow Bunburyist, eventually sniffs it all out and forces Jack to confess. What is most surprising is that Jack seems to have no shame about the lies he's been feeding to Algernon for years.

Jack: [...] When one is placed in the position of guardian, one has to adopt a very high moral tone on all subjects. It's one's duty to do so. And as a high moral tone can hardly be said to conduce very much to either one's health or one's happiness, in order to get up to town I have always pretended to have a younger brother of the name of Ernest, who lives in the Albany, and gets into the most dreadful scrapes. (I.83)

Thought: Jack reveals the reason behind his deceit. His life is torn between duty and pleasure. Being dutiful is excessively boring to Jack, so he created his younger brother, Ernest. With Ernest, he has a means of escaping the drab life of a legal guardian into the more interesting world of a social London.

Algernon: You have invented a very useful younger brother called Ernest, in order that you may be able to come up to town as often as you like. I have invented an invaluable permanent invalid called Bunbury, in order that I may be able to go down into the country whenever I choose. Bunbury is perfectly invaluable. If it wasn't for Bunbury's extraordinary bad health, for instance, I wouldn't be able to dine with you at Willis's to- night, for I have been really engaged to Aunt Augusta for more than a week. (I.88)

Thought: Bunbury is Algernon's version of Ernest. Like Jack, Algernon also uses excuses about Bunbury to get out of familial responsibilities – like dining with his Aunt Augusta. He practices deceit, like Jack, to avoid unpleasant situations and create more pleasant ones for himself.

Cecily: Miss Prism has just been complaining of a slight headache. I think it would do her so much good to have a short stroll with you in the Park, Dr. Chasuble.

Miss Prism: Cecily, I have not mentioned anything about a headache. (II.21-22)

Thought: Cecily makes up false facts to get out of doing her lessons and, to encourage a relationship between Miss Prism and Dr. Chasuble. The success of her deceit depends on her ability to read people; the fact that she does get Miss Prism and Dr. Chasuble to leave her is a testament to her powers of persuasion. Although her deceit is not as serious as Jack's or Algernon's, she lies for the same reasons – to get out of tedious or unpleasant situations. This makes her a perfect match for Algernon.

Cecily: Your brother Ernest...arrived about half an hour ago.

Jack: What nonsense! I haven't got a brother.

Cecily: Oh, don't say that. However badly he may have behaved to you in the past he is still your brother. You couldn't be so heartless as to disown him. I'll tell him to come out. And you will shake hands with him, won't you, Uncle Jack? (II.133-135)

Thought: The fact that Jack lied (and later revealed the truth) to Algernon, gave Algernon the opportunity to impersonate Ernest. Had Jack not lied, perhaps Algernon would never have had the chance to court Cecily as he did. As it stands, not only does Cecily believe in Ernest, but she's also on his side – scolding her Uncle Jack for being "so heartless as to disown him."

Jack: [Slowly and hesitatingly] Gwendolen – Cecily – it is very painful for me to be forced to speak the truth. It is the first time in my life that I have ever been reduced to such a painful position, and I am really quite inexperienced in doing anything of the kind. However, I will tell you quite frankly that I have no brother Ernest. I have no brother at all. (II.348)

Thought: An adept and habitual liar, Jack does not hold truth and honesty in high regard. Here, he comes out and says it. To him, lying is a more efficient and perhaps more noble way to live one's life. This is, of course, the opposite of conventional thinking.

Algernon: [Stammering] Oh! No! Bunbury doesn't live here. Bunbury is somewhere else at present. In fact, Bunbury is dead. (III.49)

Thought: Interestingly, Algernon lies to free himself from future lying. By killing off the fictional Bunbury, Algernon is setting himself up to speak the truth for the rest of his life. He effectively lies so that he can live a better and more ethical life with Cecily.

Cecily: Well, I am really only eighteen, but I always admit to twenty when I go to evening parties.

Lady Bracknell: You are perfectly right in making some slight alteration. Indeed, no woman should ever be quite accurate about her age. It looks so calculating . . . (III.95-96)

Thought: The fact that Cecily admits to this white lie – concealing her true age – might show that she is not ashamed of telling a fib in the first place. But it also feeds into the stereotype that many women might try to seem younger and more beautiful in social situations. Here, Cecily wants to create the illusion that she is more mature, worldly, and perhaps more suitable as a prospective wife.

Jack: The Army Lists of the last forty years are here. These delightful records should have been my constant study. [Rushes to bookcase and tears the books out.] M. Generals . . . Mallam, Maxbohm, Magley, what ghastly names they have - Markby, Migsby, Mobbs, Moncrieff! Lieutenant 1840, Captain, Lieutenant-Colonel, Colonel, General 1869, Christian names, Ernest John. [Puts book very quietly down and speaks quite calmly.] I always told you, Gwendolen, my name was Ernest, didn't I? Well, it is Ernest after all. I mean it naturally is Ernest. (III.170)

Thought: This is perhaps the most ironic revelation of the whole play. It shows that Jack has not been lying this entire time to Gwendolen. His name really is Ernest. The pun comes into play. Jack has been earnest about being Ernest.

Lady Bracknell: My nephew, you seem to be displaying signs of triviality.

Jack: On the contrary, Aunt Augusta, I've now realised for the first time in my life the vital Importance of Being Earnest. (III.180-181)

Thought: Despite Jack's statement that he's learned the "Importance of Being Earnest" or the importance of being honest, we must question his sincerity. Because we realize that there is a pun between the adjective earnest and the proper name, Ernest, we can interpret Jack's comment as tongue-in-cheek. He was accidentally truthful in telling Gwendolen his name was Ernest. But he was still untruthful about his younger brother being named Ernest. So in this way, Jack is both earnest and deceitful for the duration of the play. So what does Jack mean here? The importance of being honest? Or the importance of being named Ernest?

Marriage Quotes

Algernon: Why is it that at a bachelor's establishment the servants invariably drink the champagne? I ask merely for information.

Lane: I attribute it to the superior quality of the wine, sir. I have often observed that in married households the champagne is rarely of a first-rate brand.

Algernon: Good heavens! Is marriage so demoralising as that?

Lane: I believe it is a very pleasant state, sir. I have had very little experience of it myself up to the present. I have only been married once. That was in consequence of a misunderstanding between myself and a young person. (I.9-12)

Thought: The question here is whether or not marriage is demoralizing. This is one of the main questions that keeps popping up throughout the play. Lane doesn't think that marriage is "demoralizing." But Lane's opinions are questionable since his marriage did not succeed.

Jack: I am in love with Gwendolen. I have come up to town expressly to propose to her.

Algernon: I thought you had come up for pleasure? . . . I call that business.

Jack: How utterly unromantic you are! (I.36-38)

Thought: Algernon seems to think that proposal and marriage are items of "business," and not "pleasure." He thinks of marriage as a social obligation he must fulfill in order to maintain a respectable name. Jack, on the other hand, has a much more positive view of marriage (possibly because he's already met the love of his life); he seems to regard marriage as romantic.

Algernon: Nothing will induce me to part with Bunbury, and if you ever get married, which seems to me extremely problematic, you will be very glad to know Bunbury. A man who marries without knowing Bunbury has a very tedious time of it.

Jack: That is nonsense. If I marry a charming girl like Gwendolen, and she is the only girl I ever saw in my life that I would marry, I certainly won't want to know Bunbury.

Algernon: Then your wife will. You don't seem to realise, that in married life three is company and two is none. (I.94-96)

Thought: Algernon's skepticism about marriage is revealed in his comments about Bunbury. The fictional character, Bunbury, is used as an excuse for a person to get out of his responsibilities. The fact that he thinks Bunbury will be a useful tool for a husband or wife might reveal that he does not think couples are faithful to each other after matrimony. In contrast, Jack thinks that married couples can be perfectly happy and faithful to each other.

Gwendolen: I adore you [Jack]. But you haven't proposed to me yet. Nothing has been said at all about marriage. The subject has not even been touched on. (I.157)

Thought: Gwendolen's comments reveal that she thinks marriages (and proposals) should be organized. Her insistence on a proper proposal also reveals her coy nature.

Lady Bracknell: Pardon me, you are not engaged to any one. When you do become engaged to some one, I, or your father, should his health permit him, will inform you of the fact. An engagement should come on a young girl as a surprise, pleasant or unpleasant, as the case may be. It is hardly a matter that she could be allowed to arrange for herself . . . And now I have a few questions to put to you, Mr. Worthing. (I.172)

Thought: It is obvious from these comments that Lady Bracknell's idea of marriage differs greatly from Gwendolen's. While Gwendolen believes that a girl should be able to fall in love and marry the man of her choice, regardless of his social class, Lady Bracknell thinks that love should have nothing to do with it. In fact, she thinks that it's okay for a girl not to even meet her future husband before marrying him. Lady Bracknell's concept of marriage is based on the idea that it must be – above all – a mark of social status.

Lady Bracknell: You can hardly imagine that I and Lord Bracknell would dream of allowing our only daughter - a girl brought up with the utmost care - to marry into a cloak-room, and form an alliance with a parcel? Good morning, Mr. Worthing! (I.218)

Thought: Since Lady Bracknell thinks that a woman should marry to improve her social status, it makes sense that she would blast Jack, for not knowing anything about his family. She can't imagine any honorable man dreaming of proposing to her daughter without having any noble connections.

Miss Prism: You are too much alone, dear Dr. Chasuble. You should get married. A misanthrope I can understand - a womanthrope, never!

Chasuble: [With a scholar's shudder] Believe me, I do not deserve so neologistic a phrase. The precept as well as the practice of the Primitive Church was distinctly against matrimony.

Miss Prism: [Sententiously] That is obviously the reason why the Primitive Church has not lasted up to the present day. And you do not seem to realise, dear Doctor, that by persistently remaining single, a man converts himself into a permanent public temptation. Men should be more careful; this very celibacy leads weaker vessels astray.

Chasuble: But is a man not equally attractive when married?

Miss Prism: No married man is ever attractive except to his wife.

Chasuble: And often, I've been told, not even to her.

Miss Prism: That depends on the intellectual sympathies of the woman. Maturity can always be depended on. Ripeness can be trusted. Young women are green. (II.81-87)

Thought: Here, we see yet another opinion on marriage – this time from two respectable, and more mature individuals, Miss Prism and Dr. Chasuble. Miss Prism's comments reveal her belief that all respectable men should get married. Her logic is as follows: bachelors permanently become temptations for women if they stay single. Thus, it is their duty to stop leading women astray. Her comment that "young women are green" suggests that women should wait to marry until they are mature enough to value their husbands.

Chasuble: Your brother was, I believe, unmarried, was he not?

Jack: Oh yes.

Miss Prism: [Bitterly] People who live entirely for pleasure usually are. (II.113-115)

Thought: Miss Prism – like Algernon – differentiates between business and pleasure. But she differs from Algernon in that she embraces responsibility and duty. So while she believes that marriage is a social responsibility, she considers it an honor and a mark of respect.

Algernon: But why on earth did you break it off? What had I done? I had done nothing at all. Cecily, I am very much hurt indeed to hear you broke it off. Particularly when the weather was so charming.

Cecily: It would hardly have been a really serious engagement if it hadn't been broken off at least once. But I forgave you before the week was out. (II.224-225)

Thought: Cecily's comment that "it would hardly have been a really serious engagement if it hadn't been broken off at least once" hints that she thinks marriage is a big deal. But, because Cecily is so young and believes in happily-ever-afters, she has not quite grasped the seriousness of marriage to the extent that Lady Bracknell or Miss Prism have.

Lady Bracknell: To speak frankly, I am not in favour of long engagements. They give people the opportunity of finding out each other's character before marriage, which I think is never advisable. (III.86)

Thought: That Lady Bracknell considers it "never advisable" to "give people the opportunity of finding out each other's character before marriage" just shows that high society has made the institution of marriage more about politics and less about love. A politically or socially respectable marriage has nothing to do with chemistry between the couple and everything to do with each individual's bloodlines and credentials.

Jack: [Embracing her] Yes . . . mother!

Miss Prism: [Recoiling in indignant astonishment] Mr. Worthing! I am unmarried!

Jack: Unmarried! I do not deny that is a serious blow. (III.148-150)

Thought: In the nineteenth century, it was unspeakably dishonorable for an unmarried woman to have children because it means that she has lost her virginity before her wedding night. Thus, Miss Prism is horrified that Jack would imply that she is his mother when she has no husband. Compared to social standards nowadays, the practices of the nineteenth century were harsher and more judgmental of women than they are now.

Respect and Reputation Quotes

Algernon: My dear fellow, the way you flirt with Gwendolen is perfectly disgraceful. It is almost as bad as the way Gwendolen flirts with you. (I.35)

Thought: Because girls are under such strict moral codes in the Victorian era, it is dishonorable for them to be seen flirting publicly with men, especially single men. On the flip side, it is also socially questionable for a man to be seen flirting with a woman since that would be interpreted as leading her astray.

Algernon: Well, in the first place girls never marry the men they flirt with. Girls don't think it right. (I.47)

Thought: According to Algernon, "girls never marry the men they flirt with" because "girls don't think it right." This shows that the men that women marry are different from the type of men they flirt with. Flirtation usually means that two people are attracted to each other. If girls don't marry

the men they flirt with, this means they marry men to whom they are not attracted.

Jack: ...you have no right whatsoever to read what is written inside. It is a very ungentlemanly thing to read a private cigarette case. (I.59)

Thought: Unlike Algernon, Jack has a sense of morality, which he defines as what is "gentlemanly." To Jack, it is dishonorable or "ungentlemanly" for a man to pry into another's private life. He distinguishes between the public sphere and the private in a way that Algernon does not – as evidenced by Algernon's later desire to peek into Cecily's diary.

Lady Bracknell: What is your income?

Jack: Between seven and eight thousand a year.

Lady Bracknell: [Makes a note in her book] In land, or in investments?

Jack: In investments, chiefly.

Lady Bracknell: That is satisfactory. What between the duties expected of one during one's lifetime, and the duties exacted from one after one's death, land has ceased to be either a profit or a pleasure. It gives one position, and prevents one from keeping it up. That's all that can be said about land.

Jack: I have a country house with some land, of course, attached to it, about fifteen hundred acres, I believe; but I don't depend on that for my real income. In fact, as far as I can make out, the poachers are the only people who make anything out of it.

Lady Bracknell: A country house! How many bedrooms? Well, that point can be cleared up afterwards. You have a town house, I hope? A girl with a simple, unspoiled nature, like Gwendolen, could hardly be expected to reside in the country.

Jack: Well, I own a house in Belgrave Square, but it is let by the year to Lady Bloxham. Of course, I can get it back whenever I like, at six months' notice.

Lady Bracknell: Lady Bloxham? I don't know her.

Jack: Oh, she goes about very little. She is a lady considerably advanced in years.

Lady Bracknell: Ah, nowadays that is no guarantee of respectability of character. What number in Belgrave Square?

Jack: 149.

Lady Bracknell: [Shaking her head] The unfashionable side. I thought there was something. However, that could easily be altered.

Jack: Do you mean the fashion, or the side?

Lady Bracknell: [Sternly] Both, if necessary, I presume. (I. 184-198)

Thought: What the upper class considers respectable is wealth and style. This is shown in Lady Bracknell's interest in Jack's assets when considering whether or not he is a proper suitor for Gwendolen's hand. It is also important that Jack has enough wealth to afford both a country and town house. To pass Lady Bracknell's test, Jack must live in a fashionable area in the city. Because of her pride in her rank, Lady Bracknell assumes that Jack will gladly either relocate his house to the fashionable side or change his style to reflect the current fashionable trends.

Lady Bracknell: [....] Mr. Worthing, I confess I feel somewhat bewildered by what you have just told me. To be born, or at any rate bred, in a hand bag, whether it had handles or not, seems to me to display a contempt for the ordinary decencies of family life that reminds one of the worst excesses of the French Revolution. And I presume you know what that unfortunate movement led to? As for the particular locality in which the hand bag was found, a cloak-room at a railway station might serve to conceal a social indiscretion – has probably, indeed, been used for that purpose before now – but it could hardly be regarded as an assured basis for a recognised position in good society. (I.200-214)

Thought: The most important criteria for respectability in Victorian England was one's bloodlines, especially if they were aristocratic. Lady Bracknell asks whether Jack's wealth comes from "the purple of commerce" or from "aristocracy" because the upper classes had more respect for aristocrats. That Jack has no idea who his family is, and was "found" at birth in such an unpromising place as in a hand bag at a train station immediately makes him a ridiculous prospect for marriage with Gwendolen.

Cecily: Dear Uncle Jack is so very serious! Sometimes he is so serious that I think he cannot be quite well.

Miss Prism: [Drawing herself up] Your guardian enjoys the best of health, and his gravity of demeanour is especially to be commended in one so comparatively young as he is. I know no one who has a higher sense of duty and responsibility. (II.4-5)

Thought: As an older character with a staunch sense of morality, Miss Prism admires Jack for his apparent "gravity of demeanor," especially since he is "so comparatively young" – twenty-nine years old. She admires his "sense of duty and responsibility" and espouses the same for Cecily. But young Cecily, who values pleasure and romantic love above all, sees Jack's 'respectability' as tiresome and even a sign of possible illness.

Lady Bracknell: And now that we have finally got rid of this Mr. Bunbury, may I ask, Mr. Worthing, who is that young person whose hand my nephew Algernon is now holding in what seems to me a peculiarly unnecessary manner? (III.56)

Thought: Like public flirtation, public hand holding between two unmarried individuals is highly inappropriate in the Victorian era – as Lady Bracknell makes quite clear. But the fact that Algernon and Cecily continue holding hands even after Lady Bracknell's icy comment shows that their love (or recklessness) transcends their sense of propriety.

Chasuble: Both these gentlemen have expressed a desire for immediate baptism.

Lady Bracknell: At their age? The idea is grotesque and irreligious! Algernon, I forbid you to be baptized. I will not hear of such excesses. (III.111-112)

Thought: As a noble, Lady Bracknell is conservative in her religious outlooks, even when practices such as baptizing adults are not forbidden by the Church, Lady Bracknell doesn't approve. Lady Bracknell believes that because of her high rank, she knows better than others – even clerics – what is respectable in religious practice.

Jack: [Embracing her] Yes . . . mother!

Miss Prism: [Recoiling in indignant astonishment] Mr. Worthing! I am unmarried!

Jack: Unmarried! I do not deny that is a serious blow. (III.148-150)

Thought: By Victorian standards, an unmarried mother is a most scandalous and dishonorable individual. It means that she lost her virginity before marriage. In a time when female chastity was highly valued – and indeed, used as a bargaining chip in arranging marriages – an unmarried pregnancy was not only a disgrace, but a ticket straight out of the upper social circles.

Society and Class Quotes

Algernon: Lane's views on marriage seem somewhat lax. Really, if the lower orders don't set us a good example, what on earth is the use of them? They seem, as a class, to have absolutely no sense of moral responsibility. (I.17)

Thought: In an inversion of conventional thinking, Algernon thinks lower classes should set a moral example for the upper classes like the aristocracy. Apparently, he thinks the higher classes are corrupt, but it seems as though he has no problem with its hypocrisy.

Lady Bracknell: I'm sorry if we are a little late, Algernon, but I was obliged to call on dear Lady Harbury. I hadn't been there since her poor husband's death. I never saw a woman so altered; she looks quite twenty years younger. (I.111)

Thought: Lady Bracknell's need to mention that Lady Harbury "looks quite twenty years young" "since her poor husband's death" reveals the ridiculous need to gossip.

Lady Bracknell: I'm sure the programme will be delightful, after a few expurgations. French songs I cannot possibly allow. People always seem to think that they are improper, and either look shocked, which is vulgar, or laugh, which is worse. But German sounds a thoroughly respectable language, and indeed, I believe is so. (I.132)

Thought: After French Revolution, the English aristocracy was afraid of same thing happening at home. So the English did everything in their power to suppress French influence. For Lady Bracknell, this includes omitting French music from her party programs. Her move has nothing to do with the respectability of the French language or the aesthetic value of French music – although she tries to make it sound like it does – but with the political implications that French anything carries with it.

Algernon: I love hearing my relations abused. It is the only thing that makes me put up with them at all. Relations are simply a tedious pack of people, who haven't got the remotest knowledge of how to live, nor the smallest instinct about when to die. (I.222)

Thought: Algernon's dislike of his familial relations can be seen as a comment on how the British inheritance system functions. Algernon's exaggerates the aristocratic greed for money. If his older siblings would die, Algernon could legally inherit all his father's financial assets.

Miss Prism: [Calling] Cecily, Cecily! Surely such a utilitarian occupation as the watering of flowers is rather Moulton's duty than yours? Especially at a moment when intellectual pleasures await you. Your German grammar is on the table. (II.1)

Thought: Education differentiates the higher classes from lower ones. Miss Prism insists that Cecily leave menial work to servants while concentrating on her lessons. The idea is that the more educated Cecily is, the more she will impress important men in the future and possibly improve her prospects in marriage. She could potentially marry into an aristocratic family and better her current position.

Cecily: May I offer you some tea, Miss Fairfax?

Gwendolen: [With elaborate politeness] Thank you. [Aside] Detestable girl! But I require tea!

Cecily: [Sweetly] Sugar?

Gwendolen: [Superciliously] No, thank you. Sugar is not fashionable any more. [Cecily looks angrily at her, takes up the tongs and puts four lumps of sugar into the cup.]

Cecily: [Severely] Cake or bread and butter?

Gwendolen: [In a bored manner] Bread and butter, please. Cake is rarely seen at the best houses nowadays.

Cecily: [Cuts a very large slice of cake, and puts it on the tray.] Hand that to Miss Fairfax. (II.308-314)

Thought: Cecily takes advantage of the aristocratic Gwendolen's comic obsession with fashion. To most people, it doesn't matter whether or not one puts sugar in her tea or eats bread and butter instead of cake. But to Gwendolen, these choices are important statements on one's stylishness and, ultimately, one's reputation amongst peers. Here, Cecily takes advantage of her lower birth to insult Gwendolen.

Lady Bracknell [to Gwendolen]: Sit down immediately. Hesitation of any kind is a sign of mental decay in the young, of physical weakness in the old. (III.44)

Thought: In Lady Bracknell's circle, the authority of elders is a well-established in upholding her social class. Because parents decide every aspect of their children's lives, any disobedience on a child's part can be read as a sign of. Compare this with Jack's reaction to Cecily's indiscretions; he doesn't freak out about them. He rarely orders her to let go of Algernon's hand or commands her to go back to her lessons.

Lady Bracknell: Mr. Worthing, is Miss Cardew at all connected with any of the larger railway stations in London? I merely desire information. Until yesterday I had no idea that there were any families or persons whose origin was a Terminus. [Jack looks perfectly furious, but restrains himself.] (III.61)

Thought: As a noblewoman, Lady Bracknell insults Jack – mocking his lack of knowledge about his family – to highlight the difference in their social ranks. To her, Gwendolen's marriage to Jack would result in a dead end – or a "terminus." In a clever pun, "terminus" also means a station or stop along a railroad line, so Lady Bracknell simultaneously insults Jack's social origins.

Lady Bracknell: As a matter of form, Mr. Worthing, I had better ask you if Miss Cardew has any little fortune?

Jack: Oh! about a hundred and thirty thousand pounds in the Funds. That is all. Goodbye, Lady Bracknell. So pleased to have seen you.

Lady Bracknell: [Sitting down again] A moment, Mr. Worthing. A hundred and thirty thousand

pounds! And in the Funds! Miss Cardew seems to me a most attractive young lady, now that I look at her. (III.69-71)

Thought: Jack's substantial assets, which make Cecily akin to a millionaire, force Lady Bracknell to swallow her previous insults and consider Cecily as a match for her penniless, but aristocratic nephew, Algernon.

Jack: Then I was christened! That is settled. Now, what name was I given? Let me know the worst.

Lady Bracknell: Being the eldest son you were naturally christened after your father. (III.162-163)

Thought: In the Victorian era, it was appropriate for the eldest son of a family to be named after his father. This shows how important bloodlines are. By keeping his father's first and last name, a son ensured the survival and continuation of his family name. Keep in mind that the family name is the only claim that a son has to all the wealth and rights of the aristocracy.

Gender Quotes

Lady Bracknell: Pardon me, you are not engaged to any one. When you do become engaged to some one, I, or your father, should his health permit him, will inform you of the fact. An engagement should come on a young girl as a surprise, pleasant or unpleasant, as the case may be. It is hardly a matter that she could be allowed to arrange for herself . . . And now I have a few questions to put to you, Mr. Worthing. (I.172)

Thought: Lady Bracknell's comments suggest that girls are not capable or experienced enough to prudently choose husbands.

Gwendolen: What wonderfully blue eyes you have, Ernest! They are quite, quite, blue. I hope you will always look at me just like that, especially when there are other people present. (I.167)

Thought: That Gwendolen desires Ernest to "look at [her] just like that, especially when there are other people present" reveals her as a vain woman concerned about her appearance in the eyes of others. It is also telling that Gwendolen wants men to look at her in a desirous way, as if she specifically needs the male sex to validate her.

Jack: [In a very patronising manner] My dear fellow, the truth isn't quite the sort of thing one tells to a nice, sweet, refined girl. What extraordinary ideas you have about the way to behave to a woman! (I.236)

Thought: The implication here is that women are too pampered, idealistic, and fragile to have "the truth." This explains why Jack and Algernon don't lose sleep over their lies to their beloveds. They truly believe they are protecting their women from a harsh society.

Algernon: Might I have a buttonhole first? I never have any appetite unless I have a buttonhole first.

Cecily: A Maréchal Niel? [Picks up scissors.]

Algernon: No, I'd sooner have a pink rose.

Cecily: Why? [Cuts a flower.]

Algernon: Because you are like a pink rose, Cousin Cecily.

Cecily: I don't think it can be right for you to talk to me like that. Miss Prism never says such things to me. (II.71-76)

Thought: Algernon's line about Cecily's being "like a pink rose" reveals that men flirt with women by praising their beauty. Although Cecily protests the propriety of Algernon's comment, she secretly revels in it, as can be seen in a later scene, where she copies down all of Algernon's compliments in her diary.

Gwendolen: Outside the family circle, papa, I am glad to say, is entirely unknown. I think that is quite as it should be. The home seems to me to be the proper sphere for the man. And certainly once a man begins to neglect his domestic duties he becomes painfully effeminate, does he not? And I don't like that. It makes men so very attractive. (II.266)

Thought: Here, Gwendolen is shown reversing the traditional roles of men and women. Gwendolen challenges the conventional idea that women should be the ones at home cooking, cleaning, and raising children. This is one of the few places where Wilde overtly shows that woman can occupy positions of power and usurp the traditional gender roles.

Gwendolen: [After a pause] They don't seem to notice us at all. Couldn't you cough?

Cecily: But I haven't got a cough.

Gwendolen: They're looking at us. What effrontery!

Cecily: They're approaching. That's very forward of them. (III.3-6)

Thought: This sudden solidarity in the face of dishonest men shows how quickly women can change sides. When insulted by the men they love, they are quick to turn against them, even if it means siding with former enemies. In a society where women have virtually no power, commanding a man's gaze gives women a sense of empowerment.

Lady Bracknell: Her [Gwendolen's] unhappy father is, I am glad to say, under the impression that she is attending a more than usually lengthy lecture by the University Extension Scheme on the Influence of a permanent income on Thought. I do not propose to undeceive him. Indeed I have never undeceived him on any question. I would consider it wrong. (III.44)

Thought: Lady Bracknell takes on a powerful role here by deceiving Lord Bracknell. Her claim that his daughter "is attending a more than usually lengthy lecture" instead of rendezvousing with her lover is certainly a deception. Here, we see Lady Bracknell "protecting" Lord Bracknell from the truth.

Versions of Reality: Romance Quotes

Gwendolen: For me you have always had an irresistible fascination. Even before I met you I was far from indifferent to you. [Jack looks at her in amazement.] We live, as I hope you know, Mr. Worthing, in an age of ideals. The fact is constantly mentioned in the more expensive monthly magazines, and has reached the provincial pulpits, I am told; and my ideal has always been to love some one of the name of Ernest. There is something in that name that inspires absolute confidence. The moment Algernon first mentioned to me that he had a friend called Ernest, I knew I was destined to love you. (I.141)

Thought: Gwendolen's "ideal" of loving the "name of Ernest" is not based on anything logical. Instead, her love of the name is aesthetic. As Jack amply proves, he is far from earnest and does not really deserve a name which means "honest."

Gwendolen: The story of your romantic origin, as related to me by mamma, with unpleasing comments, has naturally stirred the deeper fibres of my nature. (I.272)

Thought: Jack's mysterious origins do not seem shady or even problematic to Gwendolen, but instead feed her fantasies of a hero with all the romantic mystery of a secret history. Of course, this secret past is not romantic for the more realistic Jack or Lady Bracknell, for whom it is an impediment towards marrying Gwendolen.

Cecily: I keep a diary in order to enter the wonderful secrets of my life. If I didn't write them down, I should probably forget all about them. (II.10)

Thought: Cecily revels in her secret, romantic life where she controls everything that happens. Unsatisfied with her mundane life, where she does nothing but study, Cecily makes up a series of romantic escapades featuring her secret lover "Ernest."

Miss Prism: Do not speak slightingly of the three-volume novel, Cecily. I wrote one myself in earlier days.

Cecily: Did you really, Miss Prism? How wonderfully clever you are! I hope it did not end happily? I don't like novels that end happily. They depress me so much.

Miss Prism: The good ended happily, and the bad unhappily. That is what Fiction means. (II.13-15)

Thought: Miss Prism defines for us exactly what fictional romances mean – "the good ended happily, and the bad unhappily." This is how both Gwendolen and Cecily picture their lives ending, with happily-ever-afters. Also, the fact that Miss Prism wrote a romantic three-volume novel suggests that she was once an idealistic girl.

Cecily: You see, it [her diary] is simply a very young girl's record of her own thoughts and impressions, and consequently meant for publication. When it appears in volume form I hope you will order a copy. But pray, Ernest, don't stop. I delight in taking down from dictation. I have reached 'absolute perfection'. You can go on. I am quite ready for more. (II.198)

Thought: As we previously established, Cecily's diary is a storehouse for all of her fantasies. Before Algernon came along, they were just that – unattainable fantasies. But now that Algernon has taken on the identity of "Ernest," she is closer than ever to achieving her romanticized love.

Cecily: You must not laugh at me, darling, but it had always been a girlish dream of mine to love some one whose name was Ernest. [Algernon rises, Cecily also.] There is something in that name that seems to inspire absolute confidence. I pity any poor married woman whose husband is not called Ernest. (II.233)

Thought: Like Gwendolen, Cecily admits that "it had always been a girlish dream of mine to love someone whose name was Ernest." In fact, Cecily's next words echo verbatim Gwendolen's whimsical wish for her own Ernest. That Cecily desires exactly the same thing as Gwendolen clues us in that these two female characters are foils.

Cecily: [Very politely, rising] I am afraid you must be under some misconception. Ernest proposed to me exactly ten minutes ago. [Shows diary.]

Gwendolen: [Examines diary through her lorgnettte carefully] It is certainly very curious, for he asked me to be his wife yesterday afternoon at 5.30. If you would care to verify the incident, pray do so. [Produces diary of her own.] I never travel without my diary. One should always have something sensational to read in the train. (II.289-290)

Thought: Since both men have indulged their lovers' fantasies for an "Ernest," we see what started out as pure daydream becomes reality – and a highly disputed one at that. The way in which both women enter their proposal dates into their diaries shows that it is as unreal and whimsical to them as their previous romantic daydreams. Gwendolen puts it best when – referring to her diary – she says "one should always have something sensational to read."

Miss Prism: The plain facts of the case are these. On the morning of the day you [Lady Bracknell] mention, a day that is for ever branded on my memory, I prepared as usual to take the baby out in its perambulator. I had also with me a somewhat old, but capacious hand bag in which I had intended to place the manuscript of a work of fiction that I had written during my few unoccupied hours. In a moment of mental abstraction, for which I never can forgive myself, I deposited the manuscript in the basinette, and placed the baby in the hand bag. (III.127)

Thought: From what we know about Miss Prism's three-volume novel (which Lady Bracknell has called a "manuscript...of more than usually revolting sentimentality" (III.126)) and her definition of fiction, we can speculate that it was a romantic daydream or hope of future stardom that caused her "moment of mental abstraction" and led to the disastrous mistake. Does Wilde use Miss Prism's mistake as a warning?

Chasuble: [Looking up] It has stopped now. [The noise is redoubled.]

Lady Bracknell: I wish he would arrive at some conclusion.

Gwendolen: This suspense is terrible. I hope it will last. (III.141-143)

Thought: Gwendolen's melodramatic love for suspense reveals how she takes her favorite scenes from novels and applies them to real life.

Love Quotes

Algernon: I really don't see anything romantic in proposing. It is very romantic to be in love. But there is nothing romantic about a definite proposal. Why, one may be accepted. One usually is, I believe. Then the excitement is all over. The very essence of romance is uncertainty. (I.39)

Thought: To Algernon, a key ingredient in love is uncertainty. This is why he considers a marriage proposal business instead of pleasure.

Gwendolen: ... my ideal has always been to love some one of the name of Ernest. There is something in that name that inspires absolute confidence. The moment Algernon first mentioned to me that he had a friend called Ernest, I knew I was destined to love you. (I.141)

Thought: Gwendolen's love is conditional, based on something silly like what her lover's name is. She makes it clear that if his name were not Ernest, she could never love Jack. This shows that she is might be mixing up real love, which is often messy, with the idealistic romances of books.

Gwendolen: Ernest, we may never be married. From the expression on mamma's face I fear we never shall. [....] But although she may prevent us from becoming man and wife, and I may marry some one else, and marry often, nothing that she can possibly do can alter my eternal devotion to you. (I.270)

Thought: Here, Gwendolen declares her eternal love of and devotion to Ernest. Usually, it is a male character who swears his love to a girl, but in a moment of gender role reversal, Gwendolen takes on task.

Algernon: I hope, Cecily, I shall not offend you if I state quite frankly and openly that you seem to me to be in every way the visible personification of absolute perfection. (II.195)

Thought: Algernon bases his declaration of love for Cecily on her looks. This reiterates the idea that a man's love for a woman can be based initially on her physical beauty.

Algernon: Well, my own dear, sweet, loving little darling, I really can't see why you should object to the name of Algernon. It is not at all a bad name. In fact, it is rather an aristocratic name. Half of the chaps who get into the Bankruptcy Court are called Algernon. But seriously, Cecily . . . [Moving to her] . . . if my name was Algy, couldn't you love me?

Cecily: [Rising] I might respect you, Ernest, I might admire your character, but I fear that I should not be able to give you my undivided attention. (II.238-239)

Thought: Cecily, like Gwendolen, bases her love on something silly. Because of this, readers also question Cecily's love for Algernon, as they do Gwendolen's love for Jack. We wonder whether or not their love is really just adolescent infatuation.

Jack: I wanted to be engaged to Gwendolen, that is all. I love her.

Algernon: Well, I simply wanted to be engaged to Cecily. I adore her. (II.367-368)

Thought: Both Jack and Algernon confess that they practiced their deceit and briefly betrayed each other's trust simply to meet and spend time with the woman they love.

Cecily: Mr. Moncrieff, kindly answer me the following question. Why did you pretend to be my guardian's brother?

Algernon: In order that I might have an opportunity of meeting you.

Cecily: [To Gwendolen] That certainly seems a satisfactory explanation, does it not? (III.14-16)

Thought: To modern eyes, Algernon's professed love is insincere because he could not possibly have loved Cecily before he met her. But his answer to Cecily's question is simple, elegant, and appeals to her romantic nature, so it is accepted as a definitive declaration of true love.

Gwendolen: Mr. Worthing, what explanation can you offer to me for pretending to have a brother? Was it in order that you might have an opportunity of coming up to town to see me as often as possible?

Jack: Can you doubt it, Miss Fairfax? (III.19-20)

Thought: Jack's professed love for Gwendolen is a little more believable. He had actually met Gwendolen before making up his younger brother, Ernest. Where he conjured up a fictional Ernest to see her as often as possible, she deliberately disobeyed her mother and traveled all the way out into the country to see him.

Jack: But my dear Lady Bracknell, the matter is entirely in your own hands. The moment you consent to my marriage with Gwendolen, I will most gladly allow your nephew to form an alliance with my ward.

Lady Bracknell: [Rising and drawing herself up] You must be quite aware that what you propose is out of the question.

Jack: Then a passionate celibacy is all that any of us can look forward to. (III.105-107)

Thought: The fact that Lady Bracknell promptly passes up such a worthy candidate as Cecily – rich, beautiful, educated, and charming – as a wife for Algernon, simply because she doesn't want her daughter to marry Jack, shows that Lady Bracknell scoffs at love as a legitimate reason for marriage.

Foolishness and Folly Quotes

Jack: My dear Algy, you talk exactly as if you were a dentist. It is very vulgar to talk like a dentist when one isn't a dentist. It produces a false impression. (I.73)

Thought: It's the timing of this statement that makes it so funny. Jack's point seems to be that dentists don't talk like anyone else. However, Jack has just lied to Algernon about his name, knowing a person named Cecily, claiming that Cecily is a vertically-challenged aunt, and finally trying to explain why his aunt calls him "uncle." It is not Algernon who is being pretentious or hypocritical; it's really Jack.

Algernon: To begin with, I dined there on Monday, and once a week is quite enough to dine with one's own relations. In the second place, whenever I do dine there I am always treated as a member of the family, and sent down with either no woman at all, or two. In the third place, I know perfectly well whom she will place me next to, to-night. She will place me next Mary Farquhar, who always flirts with her own husband across the dinner-table. That is not very pleasant. Indeed, it is not even decent . . . and that sort of thing is enormously on the increase. The amount of women in London who flirt with their own husbands is perfectly scandalous. It looks so bad. It is simply washing one's clean linen in public. (I.92)

Thought: Algernon's protests to dining with his Aunt Augusta are funny because many of us have felt the same way about eating dinner with our families. He complains about how families treat their own family members at dinner – sending them down quite improperly with either "no woman at all, or two" – which is no fun. Algernon is most offended by the fact that the woman he'll be seated next to flirts with her own husband and nobody else. Algernon's statement is funny and foolish because he recoils at the very thing that society values.

Lady Bracknell: Well, I must say, Algernon, that I think it is high time that Mr. Bunbury made up his mind whether he was going to live or to die. This shilly-shallying with the question is absurd. Nor do I in any way approve of the modern sympathy with invalids. I consider it morbid. Illness of any kind is hardly a thing to be encouraged in others. Health is the primary duty of life. [....] I should be much obliged if you would ask Mr. Bunbury, from me, to be kind enough not to have a relapse on Saturday, for I rely on you to arrange my music for me. It is my last reception, and one wants something that will encourage conversation, particularly at the end of the season when every one has practically said whatever they had to say... (I.130)

Thought: This passage reveals Lady Bracknell's folly not just in her absolute lack of sympathy for a dying person, but because she talks about life and death as if it were just another choice one could make on a daily basis. She is indignant at Bunbury's "shilly-shallying [the Victorian equivalent of 'flip-flopping'] with the question" of whether to live or die.

Jack: May I ask you then what you would advise me to do? I need hardly say I would do anything in the world to ensure Gwendolen's happiness.

Lady Bracknell: I would strongly advise you, Mr. Worthing, to try and acquire some relations as soon as possible, and to make a definite effort to produce at any rate one parent, of either sex, before the season is quite over. (I.215-216)

Thought: The comedic timing for this line is brilliant. After coming off an emotional roller-coaster ride that ends in a broken heart, Jack is told that the only thing he may do to improve his position is to "produce at any rate one parent, of either sex, before the season is quite over." As an orphan, it's impossible for Jack to find his parents. Secondly, think about the use of the word "produce"; when referring to people, we think of reproduction as having kids. Thus, this line is contradictory both in its use of "produce" and, by making Jack's parentage seem like a choice.

Algernon: Well, I don't like your clothes. You look perfectly ridiculous in them. Why on earth don't you go up and change? It is perfectly childish to be in deep mourning for a man who is actually staying for a whole week with you in your house as a guest. I call it grotesque. (II.175)

Thought: Algernon's comments on Jack's clothes are foolish (but funny) because Jack says they're hideous and inappropriate for this occasion of happiness. But it is actually Algernon whose arrival foiled Jack's plan, and make his mourning clothes look "perfectly ridiculous."

Jack: How can you sit there, calmly eating muffins when we are in this horrible trouble, I can't make out. You seem to me to be perfectly heartless.

Algernon: Well, I can't eat muffins in an agitated manner. The butter would probably get on my cuffs. One should always eat muffins quite calmly. It is the only way to eat them.

Jack: I say it's perfectly heartless your eating muffins at all, under the circumstances.

Algernon: When I am in trouble, eating is the only thing that consoles me. Indeed, when I am in really great trouble, as any one who knows me intimately will tell you, I refuse everything except food and drink. At the present moment I am eating muffins because I am unhappy. Besides, I am particularly fond of muffins. [Rising]

Jack: [Rising] Well, that is no reason why you should eat them all in that greedy way. [Takes muffins from Algernon.]

Algernon: [Offering tea-cake] I wish you would have tea-cake instead. I don't like tea-cake. (II.373-378)

Thought: This passage is as close to slap-stick comedy as Wilde gets. First of all, it's hilarious that the men to be fight over muffins when the loves of their lives have just left them. Plus, it's just silly for grown men to be grabbing muffins from each other; they're acting like children.

Gwendolen: In matters of grave importance, style, not sincerity is the vital thing. (III.19)

Thought: Our common sense tells us that Gwendolen has it backwards. In fact, this is one of the lines that makes us question the title of the play. If "style, not sincerity is the vital thing," then what exactly is the importance of being earnest? This line encapsulates the genius of the play.

Algernon: My dear Aunt Augusta, I mean he [Bunbury] was found out! The doctors found out that Bunbury could not live, that is what I mean - so Bunbury died.

Lady Bracknell: He seems to have had great confidence in the opinion of his physicians. I am glad, however, that he made up his mind at the last to some definite course of action, and acted under proper medical advice. (III.55-56)

Thought: Algernon seems to buy into Lady Bracknell's foolish idea that life and death are a matter of choice. To get rid of Bunbury, Algernon lies that he decided to die when the physicians "found out that [he] could not live." Lady Bracknell continues the hilarity by approving that Bunbury finally "acted under proper medical advice." This shows that one of Wilde's primary comedic techniques is to turn a serious subject into something light-hearted.

Lady Bracknell: Kindly turn round, sweet child. [Cecily turns completely round.] No, the side view is what I want. [Cecily presents her profile.] Yes, quite as I expected. There are distinct social possibilities in your profile. The two weak points in our age are its want of principle and its want of profile. The chin a little higher, dear. Style largely depends on the way the chin is worn. They are worn very high, just at present. Algernon!

Algernon: Yes, Aunt Augusta!

Lady Bracknell: There are distinct social possibilities in Miss Cardew's profile. (III.73-75)

Thought: First of all, Lady Bracknell's sudden approval of Cecily is based on the young girl's inheritance. We don't think Lady Bracknell is sincere when she compliments Cecily's beauty. Secondly, it is absurd to divine "distinct social possibilities" from one's profile.

Plot Analysis

Classic Plot Analysis

Initial Situation
Hello, my name is Ernest. (Act I, lines 1-78)
For the young Victorian man, the double life is the good life. Jack and Algernon both have secret identities and activities. Up until now, they have both seamlessly gone from city life to country life, using their double identities to make things more convenient. Jack's life is about to get a lot more difficult.

Conflict
Who am I? (Act I, lines 79-300)
When Lady Bracknell finds out Jack is an orphan, she sets up the challenge of the play for Jack: find a family – and a good one, or lose Gwendolen. In the meantime, Algernon prepares to

come to Cecily as the man of her dreams, Ernest.

Complication
Ernest is dead…or is he? (Act II, lines 1-247)
To make his life easier, Jack kills off Ernest and comes home announcing that his unfortunate brother has died in Paris of a severe chill. Interestingly, Ernest has just come home. We find out that it's really Algernon and he's come to court Cecily. Enraged, Jack tries to make Algernon leave, but Algy won't leave until he has Cecily's hand in marriage.

Climax
OK, there's no Ernest. (Act II, lines 248-396)
Gwendolen's arrival makes the façade harder and harder to maintain. After a jealous spat over tea, the Gwendolen and Cecily discover the truth. There is no Ernest. One Ernest is actually Jack, and the other is actually Algernon. The women's indignation is short-lived, especially when they learn their men only lied out of love for them.

Suspense
Can we get married yet? (Act III, lines 1-108)
Everything's fine and dandy until Lady Bracknell arrives on the scene. She's still all high-and-mighty about Jack's "terminus" of a family. (III.61) But little Cecily? Worth a million bucks? Of course she's the perfect girl for Algy. Unluckily, Jack, Cecily's legal guardian, is having none of it. And guess what? Cecily doesn't come of age until she's thirty-five.

Denouement
Meet my unfortunate brother… (Act III, lines 109-155)
Miss Prism has deep dark secrets. Her novel-and-hand-bag switch has caused all this trouble. Almost thirty years ago during her daily walk, she mistakenly put baby Jack in her handbag and the novel in the stroller. She dropped off the handbag at Victoria Station, the Brighton line. So Jack does have a younger brother – Algernon!

Conclusion
I told you I was Ernest. (Act III, lines 156-181)
So we know Jack's real last name is Moncrieff, but what about his first name? Oh, named after his father? Doesn't help that everyone just called him the General. Consulting the Army List of registered Generals, that confirms Jack's real name is Ernest!Everyone can get married now.

Booker's Seven Basic Plots Analysis: Comedy

Shadow of Confusion
I'm Ernest! No, I'm Ernest!
Both Jack and Algernon impersonate a nonexistent but notoriously wicked man named Ernest for the sole purpose of meeting the women they love. It helps that Gwendolen and Cecily happen to love that name. But their romantic worlds come crashing down when the girls realize they're both engaged to Ernest Worthing.

Nightmarish Tangle

Nobody is E(a)rnest.

Caught between the furious women and a hard place, the men confess the truth. There is no Ernest. Gwendolen and Cecily leave them for having non-musical names like Jack and Algernon.

Everything Comes to Light

Nobody is E(a)rnest.

Caught between the furious women and a hard place, the boys confess the truth. There is no Ernest. The girls leave them for having non-musical names like Jack and Algernon.

Everything Comes to Light

I really am Ernest!

Gwendolen, Cecily, and Lady Bracknell forgive the men when: 1) they confess they lied to be with their beloveds, and 2) they all discover Miss Prism made a huge mistake involving a baby stroller, a book, and a handbag. Jack is not only a real aristocrat and Algernon's brother, but also named Ernest after his father. Do we hear wedding bells?

Three Act Plot Analysis

Act I

Jack's second identity is revealed to fellow Bunburyist, Algernon. Jack's name isn't really Ernest. But Jack's lack of parents makes it impossible for him to marry his beloved, Gwendolen. Lady Bracknell is stubborn like that. But Jack won't let his ladylove get away.

Act II

Algernon impersonates Ernest to woo Cecily. It works. Especially since he's named Ernest. Algernon's arrival embarrasses Jack, who's trying to explain his deception. When Gwendolen arrives, the truth is revealed. There is no Ernest and the men were just pretending. The women are angry and give them the silent treatment.

Act III

Since Jack and Algernon only lied out of love, Gwendolen and Cecily forgive them. But Lady Bracknell is a party-pooper. The only sign of hope comes with the discovery of Miss Prism's dark secret. She was the one who orphaned Jack. Jack is really Algernon's brother! And the Army Lists show that Jack's real name is Ernest.

Study Questions

1. By the end of the play, has Jack really learned the importance of being earnest? Why or why not?
2. What is each of the four main character's relationship to reality? How do they cope,

romanticize, or escape from it?

3. What is the girls' fascination with the name, Ernest? What does it have to do with their romantic idealizations? How are names used to indicate character (or not) in the play?
4. In what way might the gender roles in *Earnest* reversed?
5. What do the aristocracy in *Earnest* value? How does Wilde show that Jack and Cecily have the same kinds of values?
6. Judging by the tone in *Earnest*, what is Wilde's opinion of the aristocracy? Does he approve or disapprove of them?
7. How do the aristocrats' values clash directly with a more standard concept of respectability?
8. What is the importance of the city/country split? What qualities do city-dwellers usually have? How about country folk? Do these stereotypes work in *Earnest*?
9. What's up with all the food fights? Why are they humorous?
10. How are Miss Prism and Dr. Chasuble products of society? What does this reveal about Victorian attitudes towards education?
11. In the end, why doesn't Cecily care that Algernon's name isn't Ernest?

Characters

All Characters

Jack Worthing Character Analysis

Jack and Algy

We know what you're thinking. Which one's Jack and which one's Algernon? It's hard to keep the two characters straight. Wilde built so many echoes into their actions and dialogue that on a first read, the two men seem like the same guy. Just consider their similarities: they are well educated and well off; they are trying to get wives; they have butlers and imaginary friends.

The men also share some of the traditional protagonist's job of driving the action – both characters work hard to secure their engagements, facing the stony judgment of Lady Bracknell. Both descend on the country – essentially in disguise – to deal with the problem of Brother Ernest. Both arrange for christenings they think will bring the happy ending of marriage. And neither of them changes very much throughout the course of the play.

Why would Wilde make Jack and Algernon so much alike? Isn't an author supposed to make characters individuals? Not necessarily. And not in a parody, farce, or satire, all of which are genres that Wilde drew on for *The Importance of Being Earnest*. Wilde is making fun of the Victorian upper class, to which both Jack and Algernon belong. Making light of the obsessions

and faults of the upper class through Jack and Algernon at the same time is not only funnier, but it also makes Wilde's point that the faults are in the society, not the individual.

Throughout the play, we do see that the two characters do have individual traits, which emerge most when they bicker with each other.

Jack, the Older Brother

Even before he knows he's an older brother, Jack acts like an older brother. As a guardian to Cecily, he's used to setting down rules, even guiding curriculum, as we see in the tutoring scene with Miss Prism. Jack is bossy. In the first scene, he liberally dispenses "shoulds" to Algernon. Jack has no problem giving out one piece of advice after another: one shouldn't read a private cigarette case, shouldn't discuss modern culture, shouldn't talk like a dentist, etc.

Jack isn't any less dishonest than Algernon, but Jack is more serious about keeping up his air of respectability. When he finally comes out with the truth about Cecily, "who addresses me as her uncle from motives of respect that [Algernon] could not possibly appreciate" he takes pains to separate himself from Algernon, who is "hardly serious enough" (I.79-83).

Jack also has a bit of that older sibling control thing, enhanced with a tendency to get in bad moods when things don't go his way. Wilde describes Jack's reaction as "irritable" three times in the play – when Algernon rushes him, when Lady Bracknell quizzes him on Cecily's background, and when the same lady can't remember his father's first name. Jack is as willing as Algernon to humiliate himself to get what he wants – the entrance with him dressed all in mourning is priceless – but he's less amused when things turn out badly:

JACK
This ghastly state of things is what you call Bunburying, I suppose?
ALGERNON
Yes, and a perfectly wonderful Bunbury it is. The most wonderful Bunbury I have ever had in my life. (II.357-358)

Algernon enjoys the social game, while Jack wants results.

Jack on the Social Ladder

The men are also distinct from each other in terms of their taste in women. Jack is attracted to Gwendolen, a "sensible, intellectual girl" (I.295). Gwendolen is a sophisticated city woman, and her style and education make her desirable to Jack. So does her good name – a department in which Jack, socially speaking at least, could stand to improve. Even before Jack discovers his true origins, he has a lot to gain from marriage into the Bracknell family (though he'll have to deal with Lady Bracknell on a continual basis.)

Jack Worthing Timeline and Summary

- Jack-as-Ernest visits Algernon.

- After the cigarette case fiasco, Ernest reveals that Cecily is his ward. He explains why he is Jack in the country and Ernest in the city.
- Jack learns about Algernon's Bunburying.
- During an afternoon tea visit, Jack proposes to Gwendolen.
- Jack is interrupted and interrogated by Lady Bracknell.
- After being refused by Lady Bracknell, Jack plans to kill off Ernest.
- Jack gives Gwendolen his country address, while Algernon cleverly takes notes.
- After killing off Ernest, Jack returns to the Manor House, dressed in mourning. He explains that his brother, Ernest, died of a "severe chill."
- Jack is shocked when he discovers that his brother, Ernest is alive and well, and at the country house. Jack soon discovers that the Ernest who arrived is really Algernon.
- Jack arranges for his brother to leave.
- Jack comes out to greet Gwendolen.
- Jack and Algernon's deceit is revealed to the two girls, who seek refuge in the house.
- Left to themselves, Jack and Algernon fight over muffins.
- The two men finally enter the house to find their loves. Jack and Algernon reveal that they only lied out of love for the girls. They are immediately forgiven.
- Jack receives a visit from Lady Bracknell.
- Jack reveals Cecily's inheritance, much to Lady Bracknell's interest.
- Jack refuses to give consent for Cecily to marry Algernon unless Lady Bracknell allows him to marry Gwendolen.
- Jack hears Miss Prism's story, and begins to suspect that Miss Prism knows where he comes from.
- Jack finds the hand bag in his chambers.
- Jack first believes that Miss Prism is his mother.
- Jack discovers from Lady Bracknell that he is Algernon's older brother.
- Jack looks in the Army Lists to find his true Christian name. He discovers his name is Ernest.
- Jack hugs Gwendolen joyfully, knowing they can finally be married.
- Jack tells Lady Bracknell he has learned "the vital Importance of Being Earnest."

Algernon Moncrieff Character Analysis

Algy and Jack

Jack and Algernon certainly are a lot alike. So much so that it feels like we're writing a Siamese twin character analysis. Take a look at the first section of Jack's "Character Analysis" and come back for more Algernon-specific details.

Algernon's Dandy Ancestors

Algernon is a toned-down version of a character type Wilde enjoyed writing: the dandy. A dandy is an effeminate, educated, dedicated follower of fashion, and a flouter of conventional male duty. Today we call them metrosexuals. Appearances are very important to Algernon, especially

neckties and buttonhole flowers. He doesn't hide his vanity from Cecily, confiding that "I never have any appetite unless I have a buttonhole first" (II.71), and that Jack "has no taste in neckties at all" (II.57).

In *An Ideal Husband*, the play Wilde wrote just before this one, a similar character (with a similar girlfriend) appears. This character, Lord Goring, even has a scene with his butler that resembles Algernon's first scene with his butler, Lane. Wilde wrote that Lord Goring "plays with life," and the same can be said of Algernon. He is full of mischief. He loves champagne and he's bad with money. His glee in finding out Jack's country address is irrepressible. He falls in love with a girl and proposes to her within ten minutes. And even when things get messy, Algernon can't stop excitedly eating muffins. Algy treats life like a game, which makes reading *The Importance of Being Earnest* all the more fun for us.

Algernon and Fiction
Algernon's not one to lecture about the *status quo*, but he seems aware of the absurdities of Victorian high society. He responds by taking absolutely nothing seriously.

JACK
Oh that's nonsense Algy, you never talk anything but nonsense.
ALGERNON
Nobody ever does. (I.299-300)

Like many of the characters in the play, Algernon embraces fiction in his daily life. He creates "the invalid," Bunbury, with flair, and clearly enjoys reporting on the imaginary invalid's health to Lady Bracknell (who we suspect knows he's full of it). Algernon argues passionately for the existence of Bunbury:

Nothing will induce me to part with Bunbury, and if you ever get married, which seems to me extremely problematic, you will be very glad to know Bunbury. A man who marries without knowing Bunbury has a very tedious time of it. (I.94)

For Algernon, creating fictions is a necessity in this society. But it doesn't have to be unpleasant. It's this perspective that makes him such a good match for Cecily, who is equally whimsical. Think about it: you meet this girl for the first time, and five minutes later she's reading from her diary about your whole romantic history together. This might seem just a bit strange. But in the world of this play, and particularly for Algernon, this fantastical approach to life is just what he needs. He "buys in" to her fiction, getting upset when she comes to the part about breaking up. When we finish *The Importance of Being Earnest*, we get the sense that Algernon could not have written a better ending himself.

Algernon Moncrieff Timeline and Summary

- Algernon plays the piano badly.
- Algernon discusses the merits of wine and marriage with Lane.

- Jack-as-Ernest visits Algernon.
- Algernon discovers Jack's secret identity and reveals Bunbury.
- Algernon eats all of Lady Bracknell's cucumber sandwiches, and must make excuses to his aunt.
- Algernon distracts Lady Bracknell with his music arrangements to give Jack time to propose to Gwendolen.
- Algernon discovers Jack's country address.
- Algernon goes "Bunburying" as Ernest to meet Cecily.
- Algernon-as-Ernest flirts with Cecily and gets invited to dinner.
- Jack discovers that the man sitting in his dining room is actually Algernon.
- Algernon-as-Ernest sends away the dog-cart to flirt more with Cecily.
- Algernon-as-Ernest discovers Cecily's diary and their engagement.
- He leaves to find out about getting baptized.
- Algernon comes back to find the girls fighting over Ernest. The truth comes out, and the girls run into the house for refuge.
- Algernon and Jack fight over muffins after being stood up by the girls.
- Algernon lies to Lady Bracknell that Bunbury has died.
- Algernon watches gleefully while Aunt Augusta pronounces Cecily a worthy bride for him.
- Algernon is introduced to everyone as Jack's "unfortunate brother." (III.154)
- Algernon hugs Cecily joyfully, knowing they can finally be married.

Gwendolen Fairfax Character Analysis

Gwen and Cecily

Like the two male leads, Gwendolen and Cecily also have a lot in common. There's the Ernest thing: marrying a man named Ernest seems to be the founding principal of their lives. The two women even say it in unison: "Your Christian names are still an insuperable barrier. That is all!" (III.29) Gwendolen and Cecily both keep a diary, which they believe would pretty much stand up in a court of law as proof of whatever they say. And both are willing to fight tooth and nail to get what they want, though not in front of the servants. Neither Cecily nor Gwendolen has much of a character arc, because the absurd plot simply unfolds to their advantage. In the end, Cecily does have to make do with an "Algernon." So we guess Gwendolen wins since she alone ends up marrying an "Ernest."

Why did Oscar Wilde make them so similar? Because his main interest was satirizing the society that produced women *like* them – not the individuals themselves.

Lady Bracknell Junior

"You don't think there is any chance of Gwendolen becoming like her mother in about a hundred and fifty years, do you Algy?" (I.227) Jack asks in the first scene. Bad news, Jack. You may not be able to see beyond the blond ringlets and cute Victorian corset, but the signs are all there. Gwendolen is opinionated and forceful like her mother; she bosses Cecily around with

ease. Gwendolen also has strong ideas about social protocol, which we see in the first scene. Jack's marriage proposal has to be exactly right:

GWENDOLEN
Yes, Mr. Worthing, what have you got to say to me?
JACK
You know what I have got to say to you.
GWENDOLEN
Yes, but you don't say it.
JACK
Gwendolen, will you marry me? [Goes on his knees.]
GWENDOLEN
Of course I will, darling. How long you have been about it! I am afraid you have had very little experience in how to propose. (I.161-165)

The City Girl
Gwendolen has been raised in the city and is polished and sophisticated. She enjoys this advantage over Cecily, whom she considers a country bumpkin. There are a number of hilarious town vs. country barbs in their tea scene, the least veiled of which happens here:

CECILY
Do you suggest, Miss Fairfax, that I entrapped Ernest into an engagement? How dare you? This is no time for wearing the shallow mask of manners. When I see a spade I call it a spade.
GWENDOLEN
[Satirically.] I am glad to say that I have never seen a spade. It is obvious that our social spheres have been widely different. (II.295-29)

Based on this snippet of dialogue, it certainly looks like it's fighting time. But no – the servant Merriman enters and quickly restores calm. One woman may be country girl and the other city girl, but both know you don't let it all hang out in front of the servants.

Gwendolen Fairfax Timeline and Summary

- Gwendolen and her mother Lady Bracknell visit Algernon.
- Gwendolen stays behind with Jack-as-Ernest while Lady Bracknell goes off with Algernon.
- Gwendolen rhapsodizes on how much she loves the name "Ernest."
- Jack-as-Ernest proposes to Gwendolen. She accepts.
- Gwendolen is sent down to the carriage while her mother interviews Jack-as-Ernest.
- Gwendolen comes back and declares her undying love for Ernest.
- Gwendolen gets Jack's country address.
- Gwendolen runs away from home to the Manor House.
- Gwendolen meets Cecily. She examines her and wishes Cecily were older.
- When they learn they're both engaged to "Ernest," Gwendolen and Cecily insult each other over tea.

- Jack and Algernon arrive at the scene and the truth of their identities is revealed to the girls.
- Gwendolen and Cecily retreat to the house.
- Gwendolen and Cecily forgive the boys after they learn why they lied.
- Gwendolen flies into Jack's arms after discovering his real name is indeed Ernest.

Cecily Cardew Character Analysis

Cecily and Gwen
Yes, they're so much alike they could be sisters – and now they will be. You might want to check out "Gwen and Cecily" in Gwendolen's "Character Analysis" for more information on what the two women have in common.

Cecily the Country Girl
Part of what makes Cecily attractive to Algernon is her seeming simplicity. She's not intellectual like Gwendolen, who very early on scolds Jack, "Ah! that is clearly a metaphysical speculation, and like most metaphysical speculations has very little reference at all to the actual facts of real life, as we know them" (I.149). We can't really imagine Cecily talking about metaphysics – or facts, for that matter. Cecily does everything she can to vigorously avoid Miss Prism's attempts to educate her. She's innocent – Gwendolen might say ignorant. She waters the plants, writes in her diary, and waits for the day that Ernest will come and propose.

Cecily and Fiction
Cecily may hate German diction, but she loves stories. She gets so excited when Miss Prism reveals that she has written a three-volume novel. And Cecily describes Algernon's desires to reform himself as "Quixotic," indicating that she's read the novel by Cervantes in which a man with delusions of grandeur has numerous adventures. Like Algernon, Cecily loves a good bit of fiction – and her favorite writer is herself.

In her diary, she makes long entries recording romantic events that are entirely fictional. We love this one:

CECILY
Worn out by your entire ignorance of my existence, I determined to end the matter one way or the other, and after a long struggle with myself I accepted you under this dear old tree here. The next day I bought this little ring in your name, and this is the little bangle with the true lover's knot I promised you always to wear.
ALGERNON
Did I give you this? It's very pretty, isn't it? (II.215-216)

The comedy is in all the intricate details – the tree, the ring, the bangle with the true lover's knot – and the fact that Algernon doesn't quietly send for a straightjacket. In the fantastical comic

world of *The Importance of Being Earnest*, Algy just rolls with it. Interestingly enough, Algernon takes Cecily's eccentric behavior as yet another sign that she is the girl for him.

Not As Sweet As She Looks

Cecily may be younger, less fashionable, and less sophisticated than Gwendolen, but she can give as good as she gets. Check this out:

GWENDOLEN
Are there many interesting walks in the vicinity, Miss Cardew?
CECILY
Oh! yes! a great many. From the top of one of the hills quite close one can see five counties.
GWENDOLEN
Five counties! I don't think I should like that; I hate crowds.
CECILY
[Sweetly] I suppose that is why you live in town? [Gwendolen bites her lip, and beats her foot nervously with her parasol.]
GWENDOLEN
[Looking round] Quite a well-kept garden this is, Miss Cardew.
CECILY
So glad you like it, Miss Fairfax.
GWENDOLEN
I had no idea there were any flowers in the country.
CECILY
Oh, flowers are as common here, Miss Fairfax, as people are in London. (II.299-306)

Gwen got schooled. The girls are superficially civil here because the butler, Merriman, is setting up the tea. Neither Gwendolen nor Cecily can commence the scratching and hair-pulling in front of him. But Cecily proves that, though she may have been raised in the country, she's primed to enter London society as Algernon's wife. She's quick-witted and determined, and with the guidance of her new sister-in-law, Gwendolen, she'll be formidable. In time, we can almost see her taking on Lady Bracknell.

Cecily Cardew Timeline and Summary

- Cecily waters the roses.
- Cecily discovers that Miss Prism wrote a three-volume novel.
- Cecily lies that Miss Prism has a headache to get out of doing her German lesson. As a result, Miss Prism and Dr. Chasuble (who are crushing on each other) go on a walk together.
- Cecily meets Ernest who is really Algernon in disguise.
- Cecily flirts with Ernest and promises to reform him.
- Cecily invites Ernest in for dinner.
- Cecily reconciles Uncle Jack with 'Ernest.'
- Cecily comes back out to water the roses and ends up spending more quality time with

Ernest.

- Cecily reveals her and Ernest's love letters and engagement, which she has recorded in her diary for the past few months.
- Cecily reveals how much she loves the name Ernest.
- Cecily meets Gwendolen.
- Cecily and Gwendolen insult each other over tea once they've learned that they're both engaged to Ernest Worthing.
- Cecily and Gwendolen learn the truth from the boys – that there is no Ernest.
- Cecily and Gwendolen retire into the house to fume at the boys.
- Cecily and Gwendolen forgive the boys once they learned why they lied.
- Cecily is pronounced a worthy fiancée for Algernon by Lady Bracknell.
- Cecily and Algernon hug joyously, knowing they can finally get married.

Lady Bracknell Character Analysis

Lady Bracknell Alone

This very symmetrical play has an odd number of characters, nine. Everybody has somebody: Jack and Gwendolen, Algernon and Cecily, Miss Prism and Chasuble, Lane and Merriman. Who's left out? Lady Bracknell. She's the only character without a foil or partner. Lady Bracknell is Wilde's symbol of the dominant Victorian ethic. As such, she is the most overbearing and powerful character in the play. There is no question, from any character, that the buck stops with her. Her demand for Jack to find a good family drives the action of the play. If she says no, the answer is no – no marriage. This is a closed society, and no matter what fun the youngsters have, she's watching and judging them.

Lady Bracknell the Judge

As a symbol of the British upper crust, she passes down the rules and traditions of society, and stands in not-very-silent judgment of how the others obey them. When she enters a room, it's interrogation time:

[Pencil and note-book in hand.] I feel bound to tell you that you are not down on my list of eligible young men, although I have the same list as the dear Duchess of Bolton has. We work together, in fact. However, I am quite ready to enter your name, should your answers be what a really affectionate mother requires. Do you smoke? (I.178)

Jack says yes, and the questioning continues. It's all going pretty well until he reveals that he doesn't know who his parents are, and that he was found in a handbag. This. Will. Not. Do. Lady Bracknell snaps shut her notebook and sweeps out "in majestic indignation" (I.218).

Lady Bracknell, Protector of the Victorian Great and Good

What's so bad about Jack being found in a handbag and having no idea who his parents are? It means he has no name, no background, no class – he may be a peasant for all anyone knows.

And Lady Bracknell insists that Gwendolen shouldn't marry beneath her. Just like the American dream, the Victorian one goes up, not down. And Lady Bracknell has moved up: "When I married Lord Bracknell I had no fortune of any kind. But I never dreamed for a moment of allowing that to stand in my way" (III.77). There's no way she'll allow Jack to undo her progress.

Lady Bracknell Timeline and Summary

- Lady Bracknell and Gwendolen visit Algernon.
- Lady Bracknell expresses her disapproval over Bunbury's bad health.
- Lady Bracknell and Algernon go into the other room to inspect his music arrangements for her party, leaving Jack-as-Ernest and Gwendolen alone in the morning room.
- Lady Bracknell walks in on Jack proposing to Gwendolen.
- Lady Bracknell furiously sends Gwendolen down to the carriage.
- Lady Bracknell interviews Jack-as-Ernest, and finds his lack of parents very disturbing. She pronounces him unfit to court Gwendolen, unless he can produce his parents by the end of the season. She dismisses him.
- Lady Bracknell arrives at Jack's Manor House in the country to get Gwendolen.
- Lady Bracknell, once she has heard about Cecily's inheritance, suddenly becomes very interested in her and announces her consent to let her marry Algernon.
- Jack undercuts Lady Bracknell by refusing to give his consent to Cecily unless Lady Bracknell gives him consent to marry Gwendolen. Lady Bracknell refuses.
- Dr. Chasuble enters and Lady Bracknell hears him mention Miss Prism. She commands Miss Prism to be brought to her.
- Lady Bracknell forces Miss Prism into her confession.
- Lady Bracknell reveals that Jack is really her nephew and Algernon's older brother.
- Lady Bracknell cannot remember what Jack's father's name was – only that he was a General.
- After Jack discovers his name is really Ernest, Lady Bracknell accuses him of being trivial.

Miss Prism Character Analysis

Smarty-Pants Schoolmarm

Wilde gets a kick out of Miss Prism. His own sons had governesses that he disliked, and he seems to channel all that aggression (good-naturedly) into her character. Romantic, repressed, and in love with the country priest, Miss Prism really could be the heroine of a Victorian novel.

We first see Miss Prism in her role as educator, which she takes very seriously. As an unmarried woman in a society obsessed with marriage, Miss Prism takes her job as her identity. It gives her some status, when she normally would have none. She uses a lot of flashy

vocabulary – "utilitarian" (II.1) and "vacillating" (II.9) – and even tries to impress Dr. Chasuble with made-up words like "womanthrope" (II.81).

In Love with the Preacher

Miss Prism springs for the chance to take a walk with Dr. Chasuble. She is totally into him. His sermons, his lectures, his metaphors all make her stomach swarm with butterflies. Cecily clearly recognizes the infatuation and uses it to get out of her lessons. Miss Prism excited to even take a stroll with the preacher, but, in true Victorian style, she hides it beneath fake-scholastic references and roundabout arguments:

CHASUBLE
But is a man not equally attractive when married?
MISS PRISM
No married man is ever attractive except to his wife.
CHASUBLE
And often, I've been told, not even to her.
MISS PRISM
That depends on the intellectual sympathies of the woman. Maturity can always be depended on. Ripeness can be trusted. Young women are green. [Dr. Chasuble starts.] I spoke horticulturally. My metaphor was drawn from fruits. But where is Cecily? (II.87)

Here Miss Prism is saying that she's attracted to Dr. Chasuble, she wants to marry him, and she'll continue to be attracted to him once they're married. Oh, and stay away from those young women, they don't know anything when it comes to love. Chasuble hears what she's really saying underneath the banter – that's why he starts. She's put a toe just over the line of propriety. But she quickly recovers and reverts to governess mode, asking for Cecily. Chasuble gets enough of the message, though, to embrace her, and effectively propose at the end of the play.

Nurturing? Not so much.

Wilde gets a lot of comic mileage out of Miss Prism's lack of maternal instincts. For one thing, she is ready to wash her hands of this whole Ernest character. "After we had all been resigned to his loss, his sudden return seems to me peculiarly distressing" (II.137). Ernest seems so wayward, and Miss Prism believes that they are better off without him. And besides, he deserved it: "As a man sows, so shall he reap" (II.107).

There's also her hilariously cold reaction to Jack at the end of the play. He's just found out she owned the handbag in which he was discovered at the train station, and he runs to her:

JACK
[In a pathetic voice.] Miss Prism, more is restored to you than this hand-bag. I was the baby you placed in it.
MISS PRISM
[Amazed.] You?
JACK
[Embracing her.] Yes . . . mother!
Miss Prism: [Recoiling in indignant astonishment.] Mr. Worthing! I am unmarried! (III.146-149)

Not only unmarried, but definitely not willing to be called "mother" under any circumstances.

Miss Prism's nurturing deficit is what caused all the trouble in the first place. "Miss Prism" sounds a lot like *misprision* – the "neglect or violation of official duty by one in office" (Thanks, www.dictionary.com). Miss Prism was the absentminded babysitter so lost in fictional fantasies that she forgot about young Ernest Moncrieff in his stroller. That's a crime of misprision if we ever saw one.

Miss Prism Timeline and Summary

- Miss Prism calls Cecily to her German lesson.
- Miss Prism reveals that she wrote a three-volume novel in her youth.
- Miss Prism is convinced by Cecily to go on a walk with Dr. Chasuble.
- On their walk, Miss Prism tries to convince Dr. Chasuble that marriage is good – even for a clergyman avowed to celibacy. It's obvious they're in love.
- Jack returns early to announce the death of his brother, Ernest.
- Miss Prism and Dr. Chasuble grieve and give their condolences to Jack.
- Miss Prism praises Cecily for reconciling Jack and Ernest.
- Tired of waiting for Dr. Chasuble in the church vestry, Miss Prism comes to the Manor House, only to find an old nemesis – Lady Bracknell – waiting for her.
- Miss Prism shamefacedly admits to her crime of neglecting the Moncrieffs' child in his perambulator so many years ago.
- When Jack brings down his hand bag, Miss Prism affirms that it is hers.
- Miss Prism indignantly denies that she is Jack's mother and points him to Lady Bracknell to find out who is really is.
- Miss Prism flies into Dr. Chasuble's arms. They're going to get married.

Dr. Chasuble Character Analysis

As a clergyman, Dr. Chasuble is a natural target for the irreverent Oscar Wilde. The playwright has already lampooned the Victorian Virtues of beauty, youth, fashion, social ascendance, and education – he isn't going to leave out religious piety. Chasuble is willing to christen the two wannabe-Ernests with no questions asked. Christening is a sacrament, usually meaning "sacred," but Chasuble just seems happy to have the business.

Chasuble and Miss Prism are pretty much male and female versions of the same character: stuffy, pedantic, and celibate. Their flirtations echo each other:

Were I fortunate enough to be Miss Prism's pupil, I would hang upon her lips. [Miss Prism glares.] I spoke metaphorically. – My metaphor was drawn from bees. Ahem! (II.26)

Chasuble conceals his romantic signals to Miss Prism beneath silly, scholarly figures of speech, just as Miss Prism does later with her metaphor drawn from fruits. All this subterranean flirting pays off at the end of the play. Infected by the romantic atmosphere, Chasuble embraces his "Laetitia" and piles on an implied third engagement to the resolution.

Lane Character Analysis

Lane is Algernon's butler – and his comic sidekick in the first scene. Algernon knows his master well and is able to cover for him when, for example, all of Lady Bracknell's sandwiches disappear. Lane's ease with deceit underscores Wilde's point: everyone understands his or her role in this society, and excels at playing it.

Merriman Character Analysis

Merriman is the mirror-butler for Lane. Because everything in this play seems to be symmetrical – Merriman serves Jack in his country home. As with many butlers in Wilde's plays, he's useful for entering the scene just when a confrontation is about to escalate.

Character Roles

Protagonist
Jack Worthing
First of all, the play is named after him. We sympathize with his desire to marry Gwendolen and we watch him struggle to make himself acceptable to Lady Bracknell. However, Jack is not the perfectly virtuous hero we'd like him to be. He has very serious character flaws that include deceit and hypocrisy. But the last line of the play seems to justify his dishonesty and asks the audience to overlook his flaws in favor of his obvious charm and likeability.

Antagonist
Lady Bracknell
Everyone has a problem with her. Jack and Gwendolen are angry at her for getting in the way of their engagement. Algernon is sick and tired of her tedious dinner parties. Even Miss Prism is afraid of her. She's also the person that everyone has to please if they want to get married. Jack's entire purpose in the play is to discover his true identity in the hopes of making himself an acceptable son-in-law to Lady Bracknell.

Foil
A Note on Foils in The Importance of Being Earnest
Because the play is a satire of marriage – how individuals get together in Victorian high society – there are several pairings that exist in the relationships of *The Importance of Being Earnest*. Algernon and Jack are friends; Jack and Gwendolen are lovers; Algernon and Cecily are lovers; Gwendolen and Cecily become friends; Miss Prism and Chasuble become lovers; Lane and

Merriman are complementary servants for the two locales. Wilde – obsessed with symmetry – doesn't just set up foils like your average playwright. He creates intricate patterns of language as the characters echo and oppose each other.

Foil
Jack Worthing and Algernon Moncrieff
Could Wilde make Jack and Algernon any more similar? They're both single men out to find the girl of their dreams. They both lead morally ambiguous double lives through the nonexistent characters of Ernest and Bunbury, respectively. And they both pretend their names are Ernest to get their girl. In fact, they even repeat each other's lines:

JACK
Well, the only small satisfaction I have in the whole of this wretched business is that your friend Bunbury is quite exploded. You won't be able to run down to the country quite so often as you used to do, dear Algy. And a very good thing too.
ALGERNON
Your brother is a little off colour, isn't he, dear Jack? You won't be able to disappear to London quite so frequently as your wicked custom was. And not a bad thing either.
JACK
As for your conduct towards Miss Cardew, I must say that your taking in a sweet, simple, innocent girl like that is quite inexcusable. To say nothing of the fact that she is my ward.
ALGERNON
I can see no possible defence at all for your deceiving a brilliant, clever, thoroughly experienced young lady like Miss Fairfax. To say nothing of the fact that she is my cousin.
JACK
I wanted to be engaged to Gwendolen, that is all. I love her.
ALGERNON
Well, I simply wanted to be engaged to Cecily. I adore her. (II.363-368)

This type of repetition shows that Jack and Algernon are practically identical in both character and predicament. They've both been caught lying. Both their gals are mad at them. And they both react the same way, repeating almost word-for-word what the other just said. In the end, the big punch line that they really are brothers isn't that unexpected. With all their scheming, bickering, and making-up, they've been acting like siblings all along.

Foil
Gwendolen Fairfax and Cecily Cardew
In the same way that Jack and Algernon are foils, Gwendolen and Cecily are too. They share the same basic character traits – two romantic girls out to catch and wed their respective Prince Charmings. They are both rich. They are both beautiful. And they're both outrageously in love with the name Ernest. The only things that really differentiate the two women are Cecily's relatively younger age and sharper wit.

In the same way that the two guys echo each other, Gwendolen and Cecily repeat each other's lines, particularly in the twin scenes (in Act II) where the boys arrive and straighten out exactly who is engaged to whom. In a different way, Cecily supports Gwendolen by repeating her lines – much like cheerleaders will repeat their leader's words in a chorus:

GWENDOLEN
This dignified silence seems to produce an unpleasant effect.
CECILY
A most distasteful one.
GWENDOLEN
But we will not be the first to speak.
CECILY
Certainly not.
GWENDOLEN
Mr. Worthing, I have something very particular to ask you. Much depends on your reply.
CECILY
Gwendolen, your common sense is invaluable. Mr. Moncrieff, kindly answer me the following question. (III.9-14)

Gwendolen and Cecily's repetition here shows that they're in the same situation. Having discovered their lovers are lying, they grow angry and want to interrogate them. And although Gwendolen and Cecily are not actually revealed to be sisters in the end, they do call each other sisters in a friendly way and become sisters-in-law when *The Importance of Being Earnest* comes to a close.

Character Clues

Habits
Algernon likes to play the piano inaccurately, eat compulsively, and then lie about how there were no cucumbers at the market. Oh, and he goes Bunburying. At times, Algernon can come across as selfish and insincere. In contrast, Dr. Chasuble gives sermons and performs baptisms. He might seem to be more responsible than Algernon, but he too has his faults. He spends a great deal of time flirting with Miss Prism, when his position as a cleric clearly orders him to be celibate. So Dr. Chasuble's actions also reveal his hypocrisy. In fact, every character's actions reveal that they can be frivolous or dishonest at certain moments. But since Wilde's play is clearly a satire, it should come as no surprise that there are no absolute good or evil characters. Each character's virtues and flaws are indicative of a fairly corrupt society; it is the reader's job to differentiate just how hypocritical each character is.

Education
Ironically, the more educated a character is, the more pretentious and hypocritical he or she seems. Miss Prism and Dr. Chasuble throw around big words and discuss obscure theories. Their main function in the play is to provide comic relief. Cecily (who is Miss Prism's student) and Algernon (who describes himself as "immensely overeducated" [II.181]) both say one thing and then do exactly the opposite. In contrast, Lady Bracknell comes from humble origins and makes no pretense about adoring ignorance. She considers "the whole theory of modern education...radically unsound" (I.184). Throughout the play, she is surprisingly consistent – standing by her statement that she will not let her daughter marry a commoner.

Family Life

Jack cares for his family out in his country estate, providing a luxurious living for his ward, Cecily, and making sure she gets the best education possible. By doing this, Jack honors his guardian's will. By all accounts, he is a good 'son' – other than the whole Ernest-is-fake thing. Algernon, on the other hand, states outright he "love[s] hearing [his] relations abused" (I.222) and is constantly lying to avoid dining with them. Cecily seems to genuinely respect and love her Uncle Jack, while Gwendolen blatantly disobeys her mother. Gwendolen's behavior reflects her mother's disrespectful behavior to her family; Lady Bracknell lies to her husband and even makes him eat in solitude when he ruins her table arrangement at dinner. It seems that Wilde is making subtle character distinctions according to social class. In the world of Wilde, aristocrats tend to treat their close family and relatives poorly, while the "lower classes" – like Jack and Cecily – have more trusting and compassionate familial relationships.

Names

Many of the characters' names reflect some aspect of their personality. Lady Augusta Bracknell's name repeatedly emphasizes her nobility through the title of "Lady," and "Bracknell" which is the name of the land she owns. Miss Prism is a pun for *misprision*, which can mean either "neglect" (regarding her abandonment of baby Ernest) or "a misunderstanding" (which highlights her lack of common sense). Dr. Chasuble's name shows both that he is highly educated – having a doctorate in Divinity – and that he is a cleric. Did you know that that a chasuble is "a sleeveless outer vestment worn by the celebrant at Mass." (Thanks www.dictionary.com!) But Jack/Ernest Worthing is not earnest and arguably not worthy of Gwendolen's hand in marriage. We're thinking that name was both intentional and ironic of Wilde's part.

Literary Devices

Symbols, Imagery, Allegory

Ernest and Bunbury

The two imaginary people created by Jack and Algernon might symbolize the empty promises or deceit of the Victorian era. Not only is the character Ernest anything but earnest for the majority of the play, but he also doesn't even really exist. This makes Jack's creation of him doubly deceitful. Bunbury sounds as ridiculous and fictional as he actually is. Both of them allow Jack and Algernon to live a lie – seeming to uphold the highest moral standards, while really misbehaving without suffering any consequences. Jack takes it a bit farther since he actually impersonates his so-called good-for-nothing brother.

Even when Jack and Algernon are caught in their lies, they never suffer any real punishment. That they can both kill off their imaginary alter egos or friends without much to-do, shows Victorian society's real values. The Victorian era did not value honesty, responsibility, or compassion for the under-privileged (neither Lady Bracknell or Algernon exhibit much pity for Bunbury when he "dies"), but only style, money, and aristocracy. It is appropriate that the nonexistent characters of Ernest and Bunbury show how shallow are the Victorians' real

concerns.

The handbag in the cloakroom at Victoria Station, the Brighton line

The circumstances of Jack's abandonment symbolize both his ambiguous social status during the play, and the possibility of his upward social mobility. Interestingly, the scene has both aristocratic and common elements in it. The handbag that baby Jack was placed in is – as Miss Prism describes it – completely ordinary. Like any other well-used purse, it is worn from overuse:

MISS PRISM
Yes, here is the injury it received through the upsetting of a Gower Street omnibus in younger and happier days. Here is the stain on the lining caused by the explosion of a temperance beverage, an incident that occurred in Leamington. And here, on the lock, are my initials. (III.145)

Thus, this commonplace container contains a baby of uncommon origin. Continuing this theme of disguise, it is no coincidence that this ordinary-handbag-containing-a-baby is discovered in a cloakroom – a place where outer garments like cloaks, coats, wraps, and scarves may be hung. These pieces of apparel can all be worn to conceal one's true form, face, or identity. In the murderer-in-a-trench-coat kind of way.

Let's move onto Victoria Station. According to www.networkrail.co.uk, there were two train stations at the same site in Wilde's day – leading to two different sites. The western trail, including the Brighton line, led to the wealthier parts of London while the eastern road led to places like Chatham and Dover, which were more impoverished. The fact that baby Jack is at the intersection of these two lines literally puts him in an identity crisis. Does he come from a poor common family or a rich aristocratic one? Lady Bracknell tends to look on the negative side and judge him as common until proven noble.

But there is another, more positive way to interpret his discovery at Victoria Station. Trains are all about moving people to the places where they need to be. If we take Jack's presence at Victoria Station to be a comment on his social life, it might suggest that he will have great social mobility – have success in climbing up the social ladder to a prestigious position. This is foreshadowed by the fact that he's found specifically on the Brighton line, the road that leads to the richer parts of town. And indeed the story of *Earnest* is about Jack's social advancement. In fact, he's revealed at the end to be a true member of the aristocracy – part of the Moncrieff family – which makes him a worthy husband for another aristocrat, Gwendolen.

So the scene of Jack's orphaning contains aspects – like the ordinary handbag and the cloakroom – that make him seem common, but also hints of aristocracy – like the Brighton line – which reveal his true social identity.

Diaries and Miss Prism's Three-Volume Novel

You might wonder what the heck do Cecily's and Gwendolen's diaries have in common with Miss Prism's three-volume novel – other than the writing part. Well, the writing part is actually important. Think about what you do when you write. It's always a very personal activity, because the way you string the words together is completely your creation. It's your thoughts

that are put down onto paper. Your writing is an expression of yourself. So it's no surprise that some people want to keep their personal thoughts private. Hence, you have a diary. Many people's thoughts and desires are irrational; instead they're very idealistic.

This is the point in *The Importance of Being Earnest*. Almost any type of book or writing, with the sole exception of Jack's Army Lists, reveals someone's wishes or dreams. Cecily's diary meticulously documents her desire for a lover and future husband named Ernest. It even includes imaginary love letters. Gwendolen's diary does the same, minus the letters. Lady Bracknell's notebook keeps tabs on men who have the potential to become worthy suitors for Gwendolen's hand. Most of the content in these pieces of writing is unrealistic at best or fantastic (in the fairy-tale sense) at worst. But these thoughts are kept private.

Miss Prism's three-volume novel, on the other hand, reveals what happens when one tries to impose an impossibly idealized world onto gritty reality. Miss Prism probably wrote her novel in her younger days, when she was dazzled by other romantic and sentimental stories published in the same "triple decker" genre. Thus, her writing could have been a sort of diary, a projection of a perfect inner world – her deepest desire – put into words. But everything fell apart when she tried to publish it – pushing it into the public sphere. It caused her to forget her real responsibility – baby Ernest – while she was daydreaming about future success. She lost her job over it and was pursued by Scotland Yard. Her actions made her a criminal. And Lady Bracknell returns years later to haunt her about it.

So the diaries and three-volume novel of our female characters represent the innermost fantasies of idealistic young girls, dreams that clash directly with reality. Miss Prism puts it best with her quote: "The good end[s] happily, and the bad unhappily. That is what fiction means" (II.15). You might want to counter, that very few things actually end happily-ever-after in the real world.

Food
Every instance where food is mentioned – from the Algernon's opening discussion of wine with his servant, Lane, to the girls' insults over tea and the guys' climactic fight over muffins – is fraught with conflict. The fight over something as basic as food – something that every human being has a carnal need for– might represents another carnal desire: sex. Because the men fight over food the most (Algernon's wolfing down of the cucumber sandwiches to Lady Bracknell's distress, Jack's settling for bread and butter, Algernon's consumption of Jack's wine and muffins), we suspect that food fights are their way of expressing their sexual frustration in the face of unusually domineering women. You can't deny that Lady Bracknell exerts a tremendous amount of power. Even Gwendolen and Cecily put their male lovers in compromising positions and dictate the terms of their marriages.

Setting

London and Hertfordshire, England in the late 19th century (the Victorian era)
Usually, having two differing locales – like the lavish London of the nineteenth century and an

unspoiled countryside estate – would show readers a marked contrast. It usually goes like this: the urban center of London is the heart of England – full of business, fashion, culture, and general decadence – while quaint Hertfordshire would be an Edenic oasis where man can get close to nature and distract himself from the rush of city life.

But Wilde is parodying Victorian high society – which Jack buys into, both in London and in Hertfordshire. Indeed, both Jack's city home in the Albany and his country home display the same opulence. Thus, the distinction between the corrupt city and the innocent countryside is lost. Indeed, the same frivolous tone established in the city transfers directly over into the country estate. We don't see a contrast between the city-dwellers and the country folk; we don't see the city's concrete, marble, and soot set against the country's green groves and flower gardens. Indeed, the same luxury that defines Algernon's home on Half Moon Street (where Act I takes place) is present in Jack's Manor House. Act I and Act III are both set in separate "Morning-rooms" – the first in Algernon's London home and the other in Jack's Manor House.

Only the second act takes place outdoors among the yew groves and rose gardens. But even outdoors, Wilde doesn't emphasize the natural beauty of the place. Instead, he uses details like the flowers as ornaments – pretty little trinkets that aren't really necessary to the story, but set a flippant mood, just like Algernon's piano music does in the first act.

To emphasize this point, remember that Cecily is constantly watering the roses and that Algernon later compares Cecily to a "pink rose" (II.75). So the roses function as part of Cecily's fantasy – not only as a pretty background for her daydreams, but as a way to highlight her beauty. In another telling instance, Gwendolen tries to insult the countryside by referring to the flowers, while having tea with Cecily. Cecily turns the situation back on Gwendolen by remarking that "flowers are as common here, Miss Fairfax, as people are in London" (II.306). In the process of insulting Gwendolen, Cecily also reveals that she thinks of the flowers as inhabitants of her rural world, much like crowds of people inhabit Gwendolen's world.

Why does Wilde do this? Why can't the Manor House and its residents be simple, pure, and earnest when compared to the city-dwellers? Well, the problem is that Jack and Cecily have much the same agenda as the urban aristocrats do. They educate themselves as well as they can to improve their prospects for the future. Cecily is just as concerned about her beauty and fashion as Gwendolen is. Indeed, Cecily and Gwendolen are foils. (See "Character Roles" for more details on this.) And there's the problem that Jack is essentially the same person as Ernest. Thus, he has the same questionable morals in the city as in the country. Even the respectable Miss Prism has a shady past involved with Lady Bracknell in London. So Wilde makes the country setting just as playful and frivolous as the city one. He makes his point that Victorian nobility maintain the same values – like fashion, flirtation, and general frivolity – no matter where they are.

Narrator Point of View

Though all works of literature present the author's point of view, they don't all have a narrator or a narrative voice that ties together and presents the story. This particular piece of literature

does not have a narrator through whose eyes or voice we learn the story.

Genre

Drama, Comedy, Satire and Parody

In the most basic sense, *The Importance of Being Earnest* is a drama because it's a play. It's also a comedy, not only in the modern laugh-out-loud way, but also in the classical sense, in that it features a set of characters overcoming adversity to achieve a happy ending. *Earnest* is the classic marriage comedy, where couples fall in love, but can't be together for various reasons. However, hidden identities are revealed, class differences are resolved, families are reunited, and Lady Bracknell's consent is given to all the couples.

Earnest is also a satire because it makes fun of its characters – most of whom are members of the aristocratic class. Think about how proud Lady Bracknell is, and how fond she is of scandal. When she arrives late at Algernon's place, she explains that she was visiting Lady Harbury, who "looks quite twenty years younger" since "her poor husband's death" (I.111). Wilde constantly exaggerates the upper class's shallowness and frivolity to show the corrupt morals they provide as examples. When Lady Bracknell interrogates Jack, we learn that all she cares about is his money, his trendiness, and his family name.

Tone

Satirical

It seems that Wilde's main point in *The Importance of Being Earnest* is to criticize Victorian society by showing how shallow and hypocritical is it. What do aristocrats do all day? Play the piano, visit their scandalous neighbors, gossip about their scandalous neighbors, eat cucumber sandwiches, and make up lies to avoid dining with their relatives. What does Lady Bracknell want to see in Jack, her future son-in-law? Money, property, stylishness, and an aristocratic name. She cares little for his character. As the play goes on and we see just how shallow everyone's desires are, and we tend to laugh. Wilde does not allow his tone to get too heavy or dark. Instead, we find the characters in *The Importance of Being Earnest* amusing.

Writing Style

Humorous, Full of Epigrams

Oscar Wilde is an incredibly funny and witty writer. His humor in *The Importance of Being Earnest* relies on creating absurd situations and characters whose lack of insight causes them to respond to these situations in inappropriate ways. For example, Lady Bracknell's preoccupation with her own parties and lack of sympathy for invalids makes her react to the news of Bunbury's illness in an exaggeratedly cold manner:

LADY BRACKNELL
Well, I must say, Algernon, that I think it is high time that Mr. Bunbury made up his mind whether he was going to live or to die. This shilly-shallying with the question is absurd....I would be much obliged if you would ask Mr. Bunbury, from me, to be kind enough not to have a relapse on Saturday, for I rely on you to arrange my music for me. (I.130)

Most of us recognize that death by illness isn't a matter of conscious choice and would take pity on the dying Bunbury. Not Lady Bracknell. She's more concerned with the propriety of her music arrangements. She's frivolous, worrying about style over the life-and-death struggle of Bunbury. The entire play runs similarly – with characters responding to situations in ways that are inappropriate give the situation, either too serious or too flippant. Such exaggeration gives *Earnest* its distinctive brand of Wildean humor.

Keep an eye out, too, for Wilde's patented epigrams – succinct, witty, paradoxical sayings. They are often general reflections on life, and can be lifted straight out of the text and used on your friends. For example: "All women become like their mothers. That is their tragedy. No man does. That's his" (I.228). Wilde's ability to craft these sayings is what made him famous, and his true source of inspiration for the play. In a letter to an actor-producer friend with the scenario (hoping to get an advance, as he was in dire straits for money) Wilde admitted as much – "The real charm of the play, if it is to have charm, must be in the dialogue" (source: "Appendix: Letter to George Alexander." *The Importance of Being Earnest and Other Plays*. Ed. Michael Cordner. Oxford U, 2008).

What's Up With the Title?

The genius of this title depends on a pun between the adjective "earnest," meaning honest or sincere and the first name, "Ernest." So let's focus on the first definition.

Wait, we've already run into a problem. Not one character in the play seems to care about telling the truth – whether it's about their names, where they've been, or any other detail of his or her life. If Oscar Wilde were a predictable writer, we'd expect these crafty liars and dishonest people to get what's coming to them in the end. But, Wilde isn't that predictable. Instead, he throws in a twist that makes this play interesting, clever, and hilarious all at the same time.

Our protagonist, Jack Worthing, isn't as innocent as he first seems. At the very beginning of the play, we learn that he has created a convenient younger brother named Ernest. We don't know why he comes up with that particular name, but we're guessing Jack had a laugh or two over it. Jack, a.k.a. Ernest, fools the his lady friends, all of whom have an obsession with the name, "Ernest." Both Gwendolen and Cecily are in love with that name, based on an assumption that boys named Ernest will be as honest as the name suggest.

Here's where the other definition of "earnest" becomes relevant. Ironically, there is no character named "Ernest," but everything depends on pretending to be Ernest. Trouble ensues when Algernon (Jack's friend), who has his own version of Ernest (a friend named Bunbury), catches on to the scheme and shows up at Jack's country manor impersonating Ernest, just as Jack

decides to kill off his pesky younger brother. To summarize, we now have two different girls in love with Ernest; Ernest doesn't exist, but is being impersonated by two different guys. At one point he's supposed to be dead in Paris but is instead dining, alive and well, with Cecily. He's engaged to Gwendolen, but wait, he's engaged to Cecily too!

Finally, things start to unravel and the truth is revealed. We'd like to say the Jack and Algernon are finally being earnest, but they can't really take credit for the events that occur. When Jack's identity is finally revealed, he still doesn't know what his name actually is. But then he find's out that his real first name is Ernest. And his middle name is Jack. So he really has been "earnest" the entire time. The ending, where Jack cheekily tells Lady Bracknell, "I've realised for the first time in my life the vital importance of being earnest" (III.181) is ambiguous. Is Jack saying that he's learned the importance of being honest, or the importance in being name Ernest?

Here's the beauty in the play. Gwendolen is just as smitten with him when he's lying Ernest as when he's honest Ernest. The much-anticipated truth reveals that Jack was right all along. So much for earnestness. On the other hand, the truth earned Jack a legitimate place in the aristocracy, a younger brother, and Lady Bracknell's acceptance of him as a son-in-law (more on this later). So there's an argument to be made for telling the truth.

Now what about being named Ernest? It's just as important to be named Ernest in the end as it was in the beginning, since Gwendolen still insists on loving an "Ernest." So you could read the play either way. Either Jack really does learn the value of honesty at the end, or he simply clings tighter to the importance of being named Ernest.

What's Up With the Ending?

The Importance of Being Earnest is a comedy. It ends happily, resolving any tensions in such a way that all characters also get what they desire. This means that all secret identities are revealed and all the couples can get married in a socially acceptable way. Jack turns out not to be the son of some random rich merchant (which would anger his potential mother-in-law, Lady Bracknell), but a legitimate aristocrat. In fact, he's Lady Bracknell's nephew and Algernon's older brother. This makes him Gwendolen's cousin as well as lover. (We should note that marrying your cousin wasn't considered gross by Victorian standards, it was completely acceptable.) So Jack/Ernest and Gwendolen get together. Algernon and Cecily get married as well. To top it all off, so do Miss Laetitia Prism and Dr. Frederick Chasuble. And just when the festivities are about to start, Jack says a key line: "I've now realized for the first time in my life the vital importance of being earnest" (III.181).

What does he mean? Has he learned that he must live his life honestly? It doesn't seem like he has reformed his behavior: he doesn't apologize to Gwendolen about telling a lie. If he isn't more honest at the end than he was at the beginning, what does this line mean? Perhaps that it is (still) important to be a man named Ernest so that Gwendolen will love him? Maybe or maybe not. This last line is meant to be ambiguous. It could be interpreted either way. Check out our analysis in "What's Up with the Title? " section for a deeper view of what this last line means.

Did You Know?

Trivia

- When Wilde showed his completed play in four acts to the theatre director George Alexander, the director advised him to cut it down to three acts. The result was that a scene featuring Mr. Gribsby – a debt collector – was cut. The 2002 film version, however, includes this scene. (Source)
- On the night of *Earnest*'s debut, the Marquess of Queensbury (the father of Wilde's male lover) tried to publicly reveal the details of Wilde's private life, but was thrown out of the theatre before he could make a scene. (Source)
- In *Spiderman 2*, Mary Jane Watson plays Cecily in *Earnest* as her first play and almost forgets a line when she sees Peter Parker in the audience.
- In October 2007, a first edition manuscript of *Earnest* was donated anonymously to a charity shop in England – placed appropriately in a hand bag. (Source)
- Fans anticipated Wilde's new play so excitedly that Wilde had to give *Earnest* the working title of *Lady Lancing* to prevent any leaking of his work-in-progress. (Source)
- Various actresses have given the most famous line in *Earnest*, Lady Bracknell's "A handbag?" different spins, all inspired by Edith Evans's famous portrayal. (Source)

Steaminess Rating

PG

There's no actual sex in *The Importance of Being Earnest*. But the whole reason we have a plot is because of differing opinions on two corollaries of sex – love and marriage. We're not going to get into all the diverse and controversial opinions on these issues, but even in the prim and proper Victorian era, the name of the game is to continue one's family line. That means having babies. And we all know where those come from.

Birthing healthy babies requires that, ideally, both parents should be healthy. There's a hint of this in *Earnest*. It's in the scene when Jack and Algernon are planning to kill off Ernest. Jack, who has a creative streak, suggests they blame Ernest's 'death' on apoplexy, a kind of severe stroke. But Algernon protests, saying: "Yes, but it's hereditary my dear fellow. It's a sort of thing that runs in families. You had much better say a severe chill" (I.241). After being interrogated on every aspect of his life by Lady Bracknell, Jack quickly agrees; the last thing he needs is a hereditary disease. Lady Bracknell would be sure to sink her claws into that.

Interestingly, the characters that blurt out the most suggestive lines are the women. We think this has something to do with the reversal of traditional gender roles in the play. Consider this collection of suggestive lines and notice how all of them are spoken by women:

- *GWENDOLEN: Oh, I hope I am not [perfect, as Jack has suggested]. It would leave no room for developments, and I intend to develop in many directions.* (I.110)

- *LADY BRACKNELL: I do not approve of anything that tampers with natural ignorance. Ignorance is like a delicate exotic fruit; touch it and the bloom is gone.* (I.184)

- *MISS PRISM: And you do not seem to realise, dear Doctor, that by persistently remaining single, a man converts himself into a public temptation. Men should be more careful; this very celibacy leads weaker vessels astray.* (II.83)

- *CECILY: I might respect you, Ernest [if your name were not Ernest], I might admire your character, but I fear that I should not be able to give you my undivided attention.* (II.239)

There's lots of flirtation going on and it seems the women are inverting the typical power structure. They dictate the terms and make insinuations.

Jack and Algernon do communicate their desires, though, through food. They're constantly eating. Algernon munches on cucumber sandwiches right before his Aunt Augusta arrives. At the same time, Jack snacks on bread and butter. Later, Algernon dines with Cecily and promptly drinks Jack's favorite wine. After being rejected by the girls, Jack and Algernon fight over muffins. Back in the day, "muffins" was sometimes used as slang for female genitalia.

Allusions and Cultural References

Literature and Philosophy

- Aegeria (II.29) – a Roman mythological water nymph known for giving wisdom
- Mudie (II.12) of Mudie's Lending Library, which was largely responsible for the rise of the Victorian three-volume novel
- Cervantes, *Don Quixote* (II.66)
- New Testament, Galatians 6:7 (II.107)

Historical Figures

- Liberal Unionist (I.199)
- Tories (I.200)
- French Revolution (I.214)

- Maréchal Niel (II.72) – a species of yellow roses was named this French minister of war who conquered the Malakoff at the Siege of Sevastopol in 1855
- Anabaptists (III.115)
- Army Lists (III.168), (III, 170)

Pop Culture

- Wagner (I.100)
- "Wedding March" (I.219)
- *The Morning Post* (II.288)

Best of the Web

Movie or TV Productions
The Importance of Being Earnest, 2002
http://www.imdb.com/title/tt0278500/
The latest and most modernized version of the play, featuring Jack (Colin Firth) and Algernon (Rupert Everett) singing duets to serenade the girls, showing Gwendolen (Frances O' Connor) get tattoos of Ernest in special places, and revealing Cecily's (Reese Witherspoon) daydreams of her knight in shining armor, Sir Ernest. Dame Judi Dench plays Lady Bracknell.

Wilde, 1997
http://www.imdb.com/title/tt0120514/
A film about Oscar Wilde's life, featuring snippets from a production of *The Importance of Being Earnest*.

The Importance of Being Earnest, 1992
http://www.imdb.com/title/tt0102102/
A production of the play featuring an all black cast.

The Importance of Being Earnest, 1992
http://www.imdb.com/title/tt0104490/
An Australian production of the play, recorded in front of a live audience.

The Importance of Being Earnest, 1952
http://www.imdb.com/title/tt0044744/
One of the most definitive early versions of the play, starring Dame Edith Evans in the most famous rendering of Lady Bracknell.

Audios

LibriVox: *The Importance of Being Earnest*
http://librivox.org/the-importance-of-being-earnest-by-oscar-wilde/
A free mp3 recording of the play, performed by volunteers all over the world.

The Importance of Being Earnest Soundtrack
http://www.amazon.com/Importance-Being-Earnest-Charlie-Mole/dp/B000066AN6
The soundtrack to the 2002 movie, featuring original songs written for and sung by the characters of Jack and Algernon.

Images

Movie Poster
http://images.amazon.com/images/P/B00006JDVX.01.LZZZZZZZ.jpg
Poster for the 2002 movie, starring Colin Firth, Reese Witherspoon, Rupert Everett, Frances O'Connor, and Judi Dench.

Movie Cover
http://www.teachwithmovies.org/guides/importance-of-being-earnest-DVDcover.jpg
The Criterion Collection cover of 1952 movie.

Dame Edith Evans as Lady Bracknell
http://cache.viewimages.com/xc/3309999.jpg?v=1&c=ViewImages&k=2&d=BAA3E61C514E7E
C6E56D60FC53EDAB43A55A1E4F32AD3138
A black-and-white photo of the most famous actress in *Earnest* history as Lady Bracknell.

Documents

Earnest Manuscript
http://faculty.mercer.edu/glance_jc/english264/eng264_images/manuscripts/Wilde.jpg
One page of Oscar Wilde's original manuscript for *Earnest*.

Interview with Oscar Wilde
http://encarta.msn.com/sidebar_1741503246/interview_with_oscar_wilde.html
A rare interview with Oscar Wilde published in the St. James Gazette in January 1895 (one month before *Earnest*'s debut), right after the publication of *An Ideal Husband*. Lots on the French.

Rare Book Found in Charity Shop
http://news.bbc.co.uk/1/hi/england/staffordshire/7052476.stm
A first-edition manuscript of *Earnest* was donated anonymously to charity shop in October 2007, found – appropriately – in a handbag.

"The Oscar Sinners"
http://entertainment.timesonline.co.uk/tol/arts_and_entertainment/books/article2028245.ece
A really strange case featuring fake Wilde manuscripts and a forger named Dorian Hope.

"Displaying All Wilde's Many Sides"

http://query.nytimes.com/gst/fullpage.html?res=9C02E6D81538F931A2575AC0A9679C8B63&s
cp=5&sq=The+Importance+of+Being+Earnest&st=nyt
An article about the centenary commemoration of Wilde's death, which features some
information on original *Earnest* manuscripts.

"He Resisted Everything But Temptation"
http://query.nytimes.com/gst/fullpage.html?res=9B0DE5DB1338F934A25752C1A963948260&s
cp=8&sq=The+Importance+of+Being+Earnest&st=nyt
An article about letters discovered in 1985 from Oscar Wilde.

Frivolity's Finest Hour
http://www.time.com/time/magazine/article/0,9171,915095,00.html
A gushing review about a 1977 Independence Day debut of the play.

Websites

The Importance of Being Earnest: The Rude Mechanicals
http://www.rudemechanicals.com/earnest/
A blurb on a modern remake of *Earnest*. No longer in London and the English countryside, the
play is reset in Hollywood and Santa Barbara. All the characters are now movie stars and
August Bracknell (that's right, a man) is their director.

Colin Firth in *The Importance of Being Earnest*
http://www.firth.com/earnest.html
A fan site with lots of pictures, articles, and an interview with British actor Colin Firth, who plays
Jack Worthing in the 2002 movie. Get ready for lots of Wilde puns.

Printed in Great Britain
by Amazon.co.uk, Ltd.,
Marston Gate.